D1285508

Junior Broadway

Junior Broadway

How to Produce Musicals with Children 9 to 13

by Beverly B. Ross *and* Jean P. Durgin

670019

Jefferson & London : McFarland

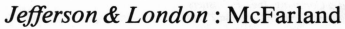

All photos (except frontispiece) by
William P. Butler and Richard J. Durgin.

Frontispiece: Annie Oakley (left) and Dolly Tate, from
Annie Get Your Gun. Photo by Jim Tingstrum, *Journal
Newspapers*.

Library of Congress Cataloguing-in-Publication Data

Ross, Beverly B., 1931–
 Junior Broadway.

 Includes index.
  1. Musical revues, comedies, etc. — Stage guides.
 2. Amateur theatricals — Production and direction.
 3. Children's plays — Presentation, etc. I. Durgin,
 Jean P., 1941–   . II. Title.
 MT955.R67 1983   782.81'07'3   82-23983

ISBN 0-89950-033-1 (pbk.)

Manufactured in the United States of America.

McFarland & Company, Inc., Publishers
Box 611, Jefferson, North Carolina 28640

This book is dedicated to
The Backstage Joy Boys
and to all the children who
have ever been a part of one of our shows

Contents

I

A Broadway Musical: Why, Who and How?

CEDAR PARK ELEMENTARY SCHOOL PRESENTS *THE MUSIC MAN*! Your eyes focus on the banner headline in the local newspaper. "Oops! Must be a misprint." Then, as you read the first paragraph, you learn that indeed young school children are actually going to try to perform a Broadway show! How absurd! Yet, as an elementary school teacher yourself, you cannot help but be interested. As you continue through the article, your interest heightens. Then you note that the show will be presented that Friday evening in a junior high school near your home. "This I have to see!" You think you know what to expect, but just in case you are wrong, you decide to attend.

On Friday night, as you drive up to the school, you behold a mini-mob scene. Where will you park? The front lot is full. For a kids' show? Maybe you have really stumbled onto something!

Seated about two-thirds of the way back from the stage in the closest seat you could find, you glance at your program. You note that all of the children in the cast are fifth graders. The list of adult helpers covers the full page insert of the program. Someone has gone to much effort at any rate. The lights dim, the curtain opens, and you gaze toward the stage.

An hour and a half later as the finale ends, you sit in your chair, stunned! All around you people are clapping and cheering. The stage is full of beaming children costumed in red taffeta tunics and matching hats trimmed with gold braid. Waves of applause roll over them! The children repeat the finale as an encore, but the audience does not quiet down. They continue clapping, now in time to the music. They rise as one to give these wondrous children the tribute of a standing ovation! As the curtain closes, the roof seems to lift from the building with the deafening roar from the audience!

1

There are goose bumps on your arms and tears in your eyes. How is it possible, this performance that you have just seen? You have clearly understood the nuance of every word of the play and every song. Fifth graders! Ten year old children!

- ► How did they do it?
- ► Who taught them such professionalism?
- ► Where did their teacher find the time?
- ► Was that two-part harmony I heard?
- ► How many weeks did they rehearse?
- ► How much did the costumes cost?
- ► How many adults helped?
- ► Did the children really paint that marvelous scenery themselves?

Perhaps the first question should be WHY should a fifth grade public school teacher put on a Broadway musical with her students? What does it offer to the teacher and to her students that makes such an undertaking worthwhile? Drama training? Voice training? A teacher has enough to keep her busy. She must give her students a proper background in math, reading, spelling and many other subjects in order to produce adults capable of coping with this modern world. Drama and singing are far down the list of essentials that an average person must learn, particularly at the elementary school level. Why, then, should she do it?

A good teacher knows that the most important thing she can give her students is a sense of self-worth and the confidence to attempt new things. Children must learn to work in a group, and no social studies or science projects can teach team work as can a play. Students — and teacher alike — must learn to organize their time efficiently when they have to balance homework with after-school rehearsals, and still allow time for piano lessons, sports, scouting and all the other activities in which they are involved. How about the students who get into mischief when they have too much time on their hands? Solution: a play will eliminate that extra time.

A teacher does not undertake a project that steals her precious after-school hours without some benefit to herself. That benefit for me is *joy*. Such a simple three-letter word, but it says it all. To see ten year old children eagerly volunteer to stay after school for 45 minutes a day, five days a week, for three to four months is an achievement in itself. To see the shy child, desperately seeking the approval of classmates yet afraid she will not gain it, finally act, sing or dance on a stage in front of several hundred people is remarkable. The self-confidence gained by young children in a project of this kind stays with them for the rest of their lives.

The popular, self-confident child is not the main winner in a play. He gains, as do all the children. Yet that child will survive in this world with a high degree of success. It is the others, those who have never felt they were the masters of their fate, who benefit most. They learn that if they put enough effort into something, they can achieve what they value most—recognition, admiration, and a sense of being able to learn and do something they never thought possible.

A teacher lives out her school career hoping to kindle a fire in just a few of the many students who pass through her classroom. To realize that one has made a true contribution by influencing others to become the best they can is a joy that keeps a teacher going. To accomplish this for an entire class of children, year after year, through a single project is simply too good to be true. Yet that is what a Broadway musical has done for my students over the last five years. Impossible, you say? Believe me, I have never found anything to come even close to the results achieved in this way.

What if you have no training in drama? What if you don't even remember ever being *in* a big play? Where do you start? This describes my feeling when I first began. A friend gave me a script of a shortened version of a past Broadway hit and after reading it I decided to give it a try. I was not seeking all the lofty objectives cited above. I simply wanted to give my children a little enrichment through a new avenue. Children are interested in themselves, and the show seemed to be a good way to capitalize on that interest. It wasn't until I started working on the project that I began to see changes in the children, benefits that I had never before considered. Since that time, our annual fifth grade play has grown, developed and become more sophisticated and polished each year. The final product these days equals or surpasses most high school productions in quality and depth, or so I have been told. To equal other productions has not been my goal. I simply wanted my students to do and be the best they possibly could, and over the last five years I have found that whatever is expected of them they will achieve.

Through this experience I have learned much. The object of this book is to share that knowledge and to help you begin a project that will have effects on your children far beyond your wildest dreams.

The Classroom Teacher's Advantage

There are many children's theater organizations in this country. Why then should the classroom teacher have such phenomenal success in working with student drama? The key is the distinct advantage she has. There is no one *better* able to coax a good performance out of children than their teacher. The key to working successfully with youngsters is a knowledge of the child and his personality and ability. The teacher deals with this daily, in all types of situations. She learns to handle each child so that he achieves at the highest level possible. This easily transfers to drama instruction. Each child is different and what works with one frequently will not work with another. During play rehearsals the teacher uses all the knowledge gained in the classroom to be a good director. She knows how to phrase a direction to a particular child to achieve the desired results. She knows the shy child and how to draw the best out of him. The discipline problems of an active child are handled daily in school, and the teacher uses the same techniques in after-school rehearsals.

The ego of a child this age is a delicate thing and can be easily damaged. Also, peer pressure is a powerful force with which to contend. A child may be embarrassed by something in the play which his character is expected to do or say. These things cannot be discussed with the whole group during a hectic play rehearsal. But the next day in class, the teacher has a captive audience when she needs to discuss a problem with the entire cast. She explains her intepretation of a play character, and why he would act in a particular way or say certain words. It is much easier for a child to perform a difficult part when he knows that his peers understand the need for doing it in the prescribed way. It is easy to save face with one's friends when one can rationalize that "This isn't my idea — I have to do what the teacher says."

A teacher sometimes makes mistakes in handling a particular child or situation in class. The chance of making a mistake is no less in a play rehearsal. However, if a teacher unintentionally embarrasses a child, it is easy to correct that situation the next day in class. Perhaps you are too demanding or harsh in a rehearsal and the child feels uncomfortable. Left to fester, the situation may go from bad to worse. But the next day in class, the teacher is able to show by her actions in dealing with the child that she does not think less of him because he had difficulty following directions during the play rehearsal. She might joke with him more than usual, or ask him to run an errand, thereby showing him as well as the entire group that "What happened yesterday at rehearsal is behind us and forgotten."

Co-directing with Another Teacher

I began doing plays in school working with another fifth grade teacher. The cast included all students of both classes. We had a script of a shortened version of a Broadway musical. There were about 23 speaking parts and 10 non-speaking parts. The other 25 children in the class would act as stage crew, props chairman, wardrobe mistress and sing in a large chorus standing on risers at the side of the stage. I had no experience at all but the other teacher had previously put on short plays with her students. We decided that she should be the Director and I should be the Assistant Director. As our rehearsals progressed, there were times when I disagreed with how she might have a child say a particular line or with her stage directions. Yet I never voiced my opinions during rehearsals because I knew that a child can obey only one director. We discussed my opinions when the two of us were alone. This is essential. Even adult professionals would have difficulty following two directors with opposing ideas.

The next year when the other teacher transferred to another school, I decided to try a play of my own. I needed an Assistant Director to handle all the details that I had taken care of the year before. Mary An, a fourth grade teacher, wanted to work with me. We would combine my fifth grade and her fourth grade classes for the show. She had no experience in drama and was happy to allow me free rein with directing. We spent hours discussing casting, stage directing, how to handle particular children with the greatest success, as well as a multitude of other details. Most of this was done over the phone during the evening because our in-school hours were full.

Mary An took charge of finding costume patterns, controlling children backstage, setting up parents' meetings, organizing the program, and so many other details. Because our show was a shortened version of one then being performed at a nearby theater, she even arranged for cast members and their parents to see the play. The trip was a highlight of the entire school year. The benefit to the children of seeing a play that they were working on was immeasurable to them and to us. Since that time, we have tried to arrange for each year's cast to see at least a semi-professional version of their play before their performance. We have usually succeeded in finding a dinner theater group in our area currently performing the play.

That year our show was extremely popular with our community. During rehearsals we saw that we had a real hit on our hands. We decided that our elementary school cafeteria and tiny stage would be inadequate for the results we hoped to achieve, as well as for the size of our expected audience. We received permission to use the larger stage at a nearby junior high school. We decided to put on a daytime performance at our school for our student body and a second Friday evening performance for the parents and community. We included the community for two reasons. Many of the cast members and their parents had friends and neighbors who were eager to see the show, and the success of the previous year's show had generated some community interest as well. When Friday night finally arrived, we were astounded to see approximately 500 people in our audience! Thank goodness we had moved to the larger auditorium!

The following year Mary An and I decided that we made a good team, and we would like to try another show. We both realized, however, that fifth graders are much more capable of handling a show of this type than were fourth graders. When an opening on the fifth grade level came up in our school, Mary An requested and received that teaching assignment. By that time we had worked together for long enough on the other play that we trusted each other's judgment, and we again produced a hit play, this time drawing an even bigger audience for our evening performance at the junior high school. We were beginning to make a reputation for ourselves, and our students were invited to perform their show for other area elementary schools. Because this involved out-of-class time, we accepted only two of the several invitations we received.

Parent and Community Helpers

During those three years and three shows, we located some willing and talented parents to help us in all areas. During our first show, the mother of one of our students agreed to serve as our musical accompanist. We did not know at the time that she had been a voice major in college, a real bonus for us! Today, five years later, Sandy still works with every show, appearing at all after-school rehearsals, holding before-school voice lessons with our soloists, and performing miracles. One year she had to transpose all of the music to a lower key for our young voices. The children and the show are so much better because of her!

Scenery is a major part of any show. Our Scenery Designer has also been with us each year since the beginning. One of Jean's first projects was designing and painting a free-standing deck of a boat. A local music store owner agreed to donate a piano crate and deliver it to school free of charge. We broke it down and reassembled it to the dimensions we needed. Then Jean painted the deck of a boat on the wooden crate. The effect was superb!

Jean felt strongly that, instead of her being solely responsible for creating the scenery, the children should have an opportunity to be involved. How to accomplish this and still have it retain a professional look was the problem. She worked out a system for achieving this. It required a monumental effort on her part, but she felt it was worthwhile to enable the children to participate. Her method, described in detail in the chapter on scenery, involved creating a huge paint-by-number backdrop, with corresponding numbered cans of paint. We turned the children loose with their paint brushes and the effect achieved was excellent. The children took such pride in the fact that they painted the backdrop themselves, and the result was something of which they could be truly proud.

Another find among the parents that first year was a Stage Manager. Anne's assignment originally was controlling the children backstage during performances, and she did a magnificent job. However, today Anne is absolutely indispensable. As our shows have become more complicated, so has her job. She is a jack-of-all-trades, and so far she seems to be the master of all of them. Over the years she made the program cover, designed and made 24 hats for band uniforms, created an elaborate Indian headdress and bustle, choreographed an Indian dance and a myriad of other tasks. All this is in addition to her monumental job backstage, not now restricted to controlling excited youngsters. She assists them in costume changes, sees that the correct props are carried on in the right places, times curtain calls, checks scenery to see that everything is in its correct place before opening the curtain, but most importantly she is our backstage counsellor for nervous children. I recall one little Indian dance soloist who was so frightened and nervous that she never would have been able to go on without Anne's support and encouragement.

The Show Goes On

During the summer after our third show, tragedy struck. Mary An, my dear friend, co-teacher and Assistant Director, was killed in an automobile accident. After recovering from the loss of a friend and the realization of what her absence would mean to the children in our school who would never have the chance to be in the class of such a caring and excellent teacher, I began to think of the play. There was simply no way I could see that I would be able to do another show alone. I knew that there was no other teacher in the school who would be willing to undertake such a task. We had built up the show, year after year, and it was now a very complicated procedure. It was, however, one with which we were familiar and would not have hesitated to continue. I returned to school in late August, eager as always for a new school year to start, but very dejected over the loss of what had become an important part of my life — the fifth grade play.

When I arrived at school that first day, our principal told me that an astounding thing had happened. Members of the community, parents of my former students, had been calling the school with offers to help me continue the show! If I ever needed proof that anyone else felt our play was of as much benefit to the children as I did, here it was! One parent sent the message that not only would she help in any way she could, but she would be at every single rehearsal, just to be on call if I needed her. Barbara became the Assistant Director for future shows. Our accompanist, Sandy, became the Musical Director, giving over 300 volunteer hours to the show the next year. Jean, the Scenery Designer and our genius-in-residence, in addition to designing the scenery, appeared at countless rehearsals, looking for props we needed for the show. She always managed to find or make them. Would you believe a butter churn made from ice cream containers and a broom handle? How about ice cream cones made of styrofoam and cardboard? Her husband even got into the act by becoming our cast photographer, building a flat so we could have more scene changes, donating and then wiring lights for the stage and so much more. Our Stage Manager, Anne, expanded her role tenfold by assuming the responsibility of infinite details to make the show a success. She combined efforts with a newcomer, Judy, to choreograph and teach dances. Our school principal was a magician at cutting red tape and made our shows better in a hundred different ways. Once I found her sitting on the floor putting rubber "feet" on our small portable stage so it wouldn't slide around during active dance numbers.

We added to our list of willing volunteers when Jo Ann, a parent who owns a printing company, offered to have our programs printed — at no cost to us! She really enjoyed working with us and the children and wanted to become even more involved. The following year she became our Costume Coordinator, researching period costumes and locating patterns that could be adapted to our needs. She served as chairman of the Costume Committee, seeing that costumes were made for those children whose parents were not able to sew. She created specialty costumes out of odds and ends. In short, she is a marvel we could not do without. Dedicated workers are necessary to the show!

So our play not only continued, but grew and blossomed. It is ideal when two teachers work together, but not impossible to do with one, especially with the help of so many wonderful and talented people. Each one has her own specialty, and each one has been caught up in the fun of working with children, expecting much from them and finding that they do not let you down. After the first year that Barbara worked as Assistant Director, she said to me, "You know, I would *pay* to be allowed to do this!"

This book is for you even if you aren't a teacher. The most necessary ingredient in an undertaking such as this is a love of working with children. If you have that and want to try a play with your group, ages 9 through 13, be they scouts, church youth or some other, we encourage you to do so. A teacher may have the advantage of knowing her children better than you do yours, and yet the results you will be able to achieve will still surpass anything else you've ever tried. So, if you have an interest, a desire and a love of children, we are happy to share with you all of the tricks we have learned in the past five years. Oh, how we *hope* that you will have as much fun as we do!

II

Choosing and Adapting a Script

If you plan to do a play during the school year, summer vacation is the ideal time to look for a script. The first prerequisite to consider in choosing a script is appropriateness for children. Because Broadway musicals are aimed primarily at adult audiences, almost every story will have parts that must be eliminated, ranging from profanity to murder. In addition, most original scripts are designed for a finished play length of at least two hours. Since this is an impossible length for young children, you must always shorten the original. There are also parts of a story line that move slowly and are, therefore, boring to children. They are best eliminated. Under the terms of your license to perform the show, you usually have the right to omit portions of the book, music and lyrics if necessary to simplify production. You will exercise this right at places in the script deemed unsuitable for young actors. Even plays aimed at general audiences will have some parts better left out.

It is also necessary to scale down the love interest in a Broadway musical. The most you can expect from 9 to 13 year olds is to hold hands at the moment in an adult performance where you would expect a kiss. Children are shy with members of the opposite sex and even hand-holding is difficult for them. Be aware of this in rehearsals. It requires special handling from you.

What Makes a Script Suitable?

Here's an example of how I adapt an original script for fifth graders. Notice that no words are changed; some are simply omitted.

10

Scene: Barnyard. Two cowboys meet.

Uncensored Version

DICK: Hey, Joe, what's a horny fella like you doin' out here sittin' in the damn mud on a Saturday night?

JOE: My girl, Crazy Beverly, has hitched herself up to that jackass Winston and gone to the square dance.

DICK: Well, don't just sit there. Let's steal ourselves a couple a' these fartin' ponies and go down to the Hot and Heavy Saloon for some wicked whiskey to drown your sorrows.

JOE: Hot damn! We'll do it!

Cleaned Up Version

DICK: Hey, Joe, what's a fella like you doin' out here sittin' on a Saturday night?

JOE: My girl, Beverly, has hitched herself up to Winston and gone to the square dance.

DICK: Well, don't just sit there. Let's go down to the Saloon.

JOE: We'll do it!

Another important prerequisite of the preferred script is the number of speaking and non-speaking parts available. Most children want to perform on stage, so a large cast is important. I prefer plays that have at least 25 speaking parts and several non-speaking parts. Few Broadway plays, however, use large numbers of actors. Professionals must be paid, and that adds to the cost of producing a play. You do not have this problem. In fact, yours is just the reverse. You *need* speaking parts.

When deciding which songs to include in your shortened version of a show, you would be wise to find out which songs are published in the vocal selections book for your show. All Broadway shows have published songs in such books. They are available from any music store that carries a wide variety of sheet music. You will find that not all of the songs from your play are in this vocal selections book. If you have your heart set on a particular song not in the book, you will have to order the full musical score for the show through the music store. It may cost four times as much as the vocal selections book and could take up to two months to arrive. You will save yourself time and money by including in your play only those songs in the vocal selections book.

Your next consideration should be the scenery requirements for the play. Try to have no more than two or three different scenery

locations and repeat those for various scenes. In one production we planned to have a train scene because it is easy to portray. The original script called for a later scene to take place aboard a boat, although the location was not essential to the story. For our show we simply changed the boat to a train and thus eliminated the necessity for another stage set. Be sure to read the chapter on scenery before you make your final decision on a script. I have filed away several appealing scripts simply because we have not yet figured out how to handle the scenery required. Perhaps someday we will have the expertise to try them.

Costumes are not a major consideration in choosing a script. While they are very important to the success of a show, most costume problems are easy to solve. Parents are quite willing, with direction and suggestions from you, to provide stage clothing for their children. They want their youngsters to shine too. Rodgers and Hammerstein's *The King and I* would require more in the way of planning and showy fabrics than would their play, *Oklahoma!* which uses outfits from the American West.

Script Sources

Where will you find suitable scripts? The public library is an excellent source because many plays have been published and are readily available. Other play scripts are available from specialized libraries that also handle licenses to perform those shows. Most will loan you a script to read and consider. When you write to them, ask for a libretto, which is the dialogue of the play and the lyrics of the songs. Purchase the music after you have decided on your play. The following list includes those libraries most likely to handle plays you will be considering. Most of them will send, free of charge, lists of plays they control.

(1) Rodgers and Hammerstein Theater Library
598 Madison Avenue, New York, N.Y. 10022

(2) Music Theater International, Inc.
1350 Avenue of the Americas, New York, N.Y. 10019

(3) Samuel French, Inc.
25 West 45th Street, New York, N.Y. 10036

(4) Baker's Plays
100 Chauncy Street, Boston, Mass. 02111

Opposite: The cast accepts thunderous applause at the finale.

Read through the libretto and decide what you are going to omit to simplify production. A show of 75 to 90 minutes is best. We have omitted songs and sometimes parts of songs that were too long, too complicated or unsuitable for children. Also, many librettos designate minor characters as simply Man, Woman, Boy or Girl. Young children need their characters to have names. I have, therefore, given each such character a name. This in no way changes what that character says in the play. It only gives the child a name with which to identify his part. Many of our children have their stage names printed on T-shirts, an indication of the name importance to them.

The Importance of Minor Roles

The children who have minor speaking parts or non-speaking parts must be made to feel important to the over-all success of the show. A technique that I have used in almost every show is to create a simple dance production number, involving 18 to 24 children. Once we had an Indian dance involving 19 children. One of these was the drummer who sat at the front corner of the stage and maintained a steady beat on a small drum, in time with the music. Our drummer felt and was very important! Our dancers and drummer were identically costumed. They were a real hit in the show. More important, they felt essential to its success! The dance became such a significant segment of the show that some of the children with major parts who were not in the dance were actually envious of those minor characters who were!

Another logical place for a routine involving many children is the finale. We like to end our shows with a flamboyant number. The children who have minor parts are used in a dance or marching-type sequence, and they end up in lines across the stage with an aisle down the middle. Then the lead characters walk through that center aisle and form a front row. The "star" of the show is the last one to walk through the aisle and is, therefore, automatically placed in the center of the front row. This is always a musical number, and the entire cast is on stage, singing its heart out at the final curtain. It always brings a roaring applause from the audience!

III

Finances and Organization

During the summer months you have reviewed many scripts and chosen the one you will use this year. You have decided which portions to omit because they are inappropriate for children.

Where Does the Money Come From?

It is now time to consider how to finance your show. For your maiden voyage on the sea of Broadway plays the major expenses will be assumed by your school. I certainly do not mean that you should go to your principal and ask for an allocation of money for your project! No matter how supportive your principal is, he would have to turn you down. School systems forever operate on tight budgets, and financing plays is not at the top of their list of essentials. Most schools do provide a certain amount for art supplies for the students. You will probably find a roll of white butcher paper in your building. Cut into lengths, taped together and painted with school tempera paint, it will make a serviceable backdrop. Painting a backdrop is a school art project—and a good one! For our schedules and programs, we use school paper and mimeograph machine.

Next you will draw on another resource—the parents of your students. They will always be happy to provide the costumes their children need, if they are reasonably priced and each child does not require too many changes of clothes. The parents of the main characters, being proud mommas and pappas, are likely to be willing to make larger investments in costumes than those of the minor characters. That is to be expected, and the main characters are always the ones with the most costume changes. So, costumes are not a financial problem for you.

In addition to costumes, parents often can provide the other things you need such as makeup, props and lights. Our makeup was donated that first year by mothers who gave us unwanted shades of powder, rouge and lipstick. Someone always has scrap lumber on hand and may be willing to donate it for scenery. We borrowed most of our props. Basements and attics are gold mines to someone involved in play production. Check yard or garage sales for items that cannot be borrowed. Expand your search by putting a notice of items needed in the PTA newsletter that goes home to the parents of all the children in school. You'll be amazed at the cooperation you receive!

The only other source for your first show is *you*. Every teacher spends his own money in the classroom because of school systems' tight budgets. I have learned to ration the other classroom expenditures and save my resources for the play. In terms of the benefit to my students, this play ranks near the top of the list, and therefore is worthy of my money. Each profession has its business expenses and the play is mine. I have never regretted a single penny put into it. Lest you be uneasy as to how much money you will need to spend, let me reassure you. My only real expense that first year was for the film and developing for our show snapshots. That consisted of about three rolls of film — not an unreasonable outlay!

Your first shows will not be as expensive to produce as later ones. One tends to spend according to the resources available. I hesitate to quote exact figures; prices fluctuate from year to year. Yet I want to stress that you should never hesitate to undertake such a project because of financial considerations. "Where there is a will there is a way!" It can be done without selling advertisements in your program and without charging an admission fee which is the way most high schools finance their dramatic productions. When the community sees your first show, they will be impressed! Consequently, next year's parents will be willing to do more for you. Our PTA recognized the worth of what we were doing. They also realized that teachers' salaries are abnormally low and they did not want me to spend my money. So they allocated $50 in their budget for our play. That was our first real financial support, and it was very welcome. Someone felt we were good enough to warrant that money, and that was as rewarding as the money itself!

Our first step into bigger expenditures came in the area of scenery. We bought large rolls of backdrop paper, rather than working with the narrower butcher paper. We also bought white latex wall paint to use as a base, tinting it with our school tempera paints. During our first show, our lights consisted of borrowed spotlights attached to an old board. For later shows we were able to purchase second-hand lights and make a permanent installation on a homemade Light Frame. Wiring and switches cost money. With increased PTA support, now up to $125, we purchased the headdress for Chief Sitting Bull in our show. It was a kit which a parent assembled for us. We also purchased feathered headband kits for all our Indian dancers. We retained the Chief's headdress for future use, but we let the dancers keep theirs. They cost only $1.25 each.

As our financial resources increased, so did our picture-taking. For our first show we took three rolls of film. For our latest one we took eight rolls. Some pictures never turn out as well as you would like, and we were determined to document our wonderful show with plenty of good snapshots. When the children ordered and paid for 488 prints of them, we knew they felt as we did.

If we had more money, I am sure we would find a way to use it. Yet today our shows are quite elaborate, and our audiences probably think they are expensive to produce. The financial load is shared by so many that it is a burden to no one. We really prefer to borrow than buy whenever possible. When we do buy, we then have a storage problem. You always accumulate a few things for each show, and as the years roll by, it adds up to quite a collection. There is no place in our school to store the equipment such as scenery, lights, costumes, etc. and my basement at home is becoming crowded!

The Parents' Meeting

September is busy with the beginning of a school year. You have no time to be actively involved in play production. In your role as classroom teacher, you are constantly assessing your students, their interests, abilities and personalities. You use this information in your daily job of being their teacher. You are also mentally storing information that will be useful to you in casting a play and in developing realistic characters.

As October rolls around, you begin to think of the play. One of your first jobs is to tap the talents of the parents. Send home a letter detailing the fact that you will endeavor to put on a Broadway musical in collaboration with your students. Stress that, although the children will be the actors, at their age they cannot be expected to handle alone all the backstage details necessary to a successful play—and you are aiming for a smashing success! You emphasize that this will be a project involving primarily after-school hours. *No academics will suffer because of the play!* This project is *extra* enrichment!

In your letter tell them the name of the play and the fact that all children who participate in auditions will be guaranteed a speaking part. Mention that *each* child will participate, whether on stage or behind the scenes. Do not even consider the child who does not *want* to participate. I have never found a single youngster in that category, and I have now spent many years in this venture!

The key phrase in your letter is: "An undertaking of this size is impossible without much parent help." List some of your needs, such as a Costume Committee, Scenery Designer and helpers, a makeup crew to apply makeup to between 30 and 40 children's faces, and so on.

Every situation will have its own set of special requirements. The stage and auditorium in our school are far too small for our cast and for the size of our anticipated audience. We use the facilities at a local junior high school. We need to practice on that stage a few times. We have to have parent drivers willing to transport children to and from the junior high school for three rehearsals. If we perform for other area elementary schools, parent volunteers are needed to transport children, scenery and props. Adjust your list to suit your particular needs. My letter to the parents of my students goes something like this.

Dear Parents,

We have decided to try something new this year! How would you react to the idea of your child participating in a shortened version of a real Broadway play? I am convinced that such an undertaking is possible for fifth grade students, and the children agree with me! We have decided to perform *Annie Get Your Gun*, music and lyrics by Irving Berlin, book by Herbert and Dorothy Fields.

I have spent several weeks this summer with the original script, which is too long for children this age. I have, therefore, cut parts of it to make it a more manageable size for us. It has been necessary to omit several songs, but we have included most of the music from the original show.

Every single child in class will participate in our show, whether on stage or behind the scenes. We will hold auditions in early December, and rehearsals will begin when we return from the winter vacation. We plan to present our show to our parents and members of the community in late March or early April. We have allowed this length of time to work on the play because it will be almost entirely an after-school activity. We plan to use very little classroom time, so that no child's academic progress will suffer as we work on our show. School is our first priority. This other activity, however, will be enriching for the children. They are very excited about it, as am I!

An undertaking of this size would be impossible without much parent help. We would like to hold a parents' meeting on Monday,

October 15, in Room 19 of Cedar Park School, for the purpose of organizing committees, discussing costumes, props, scenery, etc. We would appreciate your support and ideas at that meeting if you are able to attend. Please fill out the attached form if you are able to help us, and return it to school with your child.

Sincerely,
Beverly Ross

PLEASE FILL OUT THIS FORM AND RETURN IT TO SCHOOL.

I _____ be able to attend the parents' meeting on
(will, will not)
Monday, October 15, at 3:00 p.m. in Room 19.

I _____ need help from the costume committee in
(will, will not)
making my child's costume. (Our costume committee will be happy to assist those parents who are unable to sew.)

I am interested in helping with the following:

_____ Musical Accompanist

_____ Scenery Designer

_____ Costumes

_____ Makeup

_____ Transportation of children

_____ Dance helpers (helping children to learn dances)

_____ Helpers in painting scenery (please send in 1 lb. coffee cans with plastic lids for paint)

_____ Backstage supervision of children during Dress Rehearsals and Performances

_____ Transportation of props and scenery (station wagon or van needed)

_____ Typing and Program

_____ Carpentry (we need someone to build us a simple flat on which to hang scenery)

_____ Cast party (organizing refreshments and room decorations)

_____ Other (specify)

Child's name_____

Parent signature _____

At the meeting, begin by telling the parents about the plans you have already made. This is to be a joint teacher-child-parent effort and they have a right to be kept informed on all details. *Be sure* to let your enthusiasm show! There's one thing about enthusiasm — it's very contagious! If the parents are excited about the play, your job will be so much easier. Then begin recruiting.

If your play is a musical and your school music teacher cannot serve as your accompanist, your first task is to find a competent and dedicated parent who will fill this role. In this I was extremely lucky. I found not only a talented musician, but one who was also an experienced voice coach. In the beginning she served as accompanist only. As the years and the shows went on, she took it upon herself to train young singers to handle song phrasing, breathing and diction. She even taught those youngsters how to get more volume through exercises that they performed daily at home. Read the chapter on Music which explains many of her techniques.

Your next job is to find a parent who is an artist and is willing to help you with the scenery. The finest play in the world lacks something special without the proper scenery. Prior to the meeting ask your students whose parents paint. Weekend painters may be too shy to volunteer this information but your students may give you a lead. I found a talented artist among my parents during the meeting for the first play I ever produced. She has been able to come up with ideas for scenery to fit the most complicated situations. The magic of her talent is demonstrated best when one sees how a single backdrop can be adapted to several totally different settings. Be sure to study the chapter on Scenery where her ideas are explained and illustrated.

If you are co-directing with another teacher, your Assistant Director will probably serve as Stage Manager. If you are directing solo, find two or three patient and confident souls who can withstand the rigors of backstage discipline of excited children while assisting with costume changes, props, scenery, lights, curtain and any unexpected problems.

The next thing you need is a volunteer to head each committee. The Makeup Chairman's job is to call the members of the makeup crew and schedule them to work before each dress rehearsal and performance. Be sure to have the Makeup Chairman read the chapter on Costumes and Makeup. The Costume Chairman and her committee of seamstresses is in charge of making costumes for any child whose parent cannot sew. For our production of *Annie Get Your Gun* this committee was responsible for 19 Indian dancers' costumes. They purchased and cut out the fabric from a master pattern. The fabric pieces and sewing directions were sent home with every dancer whose parent was able to sew the costume. The others were made by the committee. Another year they brought sewing machines to school one evening and, in assembly line fashion, put together six dresses made from the same pattern but in different colors. One person sewed darts, another did seams, and someone else was in charge of ruffles or collars. It worked very well, and we had fun doing it together. The Costume chapter will give you ideas.

Do you need a qualified choreographer? Each of our plays has had at least one dance in it, and many have had two or more. Only one of those was choreographed by a dancer! In fact, the non-dancer has an advantage. She does not have a head full of ideas for dances which could easily become too complicated for children. Someone who knows less will probably be able to come up with steps more in line with the ability of untrained children. We found a volunteer at our parents' meeting and she did an excellent job of working out a dance routine. Then others joined her in teaching the dance to the children later. If you have no one willing to make up a dance, try it yourself. It isn't difficult and others may be willing to teach the dance once it is planned. There are several basic steps that are easy for children, and they are described in the chapter on Dance. Once I had a student in my class who was a fine ballerina. She was thrilled when I asked her to choreograph a short dance number for three little girls. She even persuaded her dance teacher to help.

Each show has its own requirements in the way of props. Many unusual needs can be filled at the parents' meeting. One year we needed a saddle that was light enough for a ten year old child to carry. A parent was able to borrow a pony saddle for us. Another parent located two Indian blankets and an authentic Nazi armband.

At parents' meetings we have found a volunteer who would handle our programs for us, a volunteer to head a committee to plan the cast party, and a chairman for our Transportation Committee who would call drivers whenever we needed them. Every show needs a little carpentry. Look for a volunteer father. We also located a father who had an excellent camera who would serve as cast photographer — a very important job. He even took off work on Dress Rehearsal Day to take pictures of the show when he could move freely and not have to worry about an audience getting in his way and vice versa. He still works with us, also taking pictures at our evening performance at the junior high school and candid shots behind the scenes.

Sometimes you find help in areas you haven't considered. We discovered a father who had done some drama in college. He offered to work with any children who had special problems. He became our diction coach. There are always a few diction problems when working with children. He worked with youngsters at his house on evenings and weekends. I gave him one very special challenge. A tall, beautiful, very feminine girl was playing the part of an Indian chief. I asked our diction coach to teach her how to act like a man. He blinked, he gulped, he thought, and he did it! I'll never know how.

In addition to getting volunteers for all those little jobs that you will never have time to oversee, you accomplish another purpose with your parents' meeting. You let them see that such an undertaking as a Broadway show is not impossible, even for ten year old children. They catch your enthusiasm, which is of the utmost importance to you. There will always be a few parents willing to do the minimum required, but you will also find those who will be the backbone of your show. They will have so much fun that they will volunteer to help you again next year, even though they have no child in fifth grade. You will learn whom to call when an unforeseen problem arises — those always willing to take on one more job.

Presenting the Script

By mid-November your students are eager to begin work on the play. Give each child a script. Caution him that it is the only one he will be given. I always staple every script into a manila folder, and on the front I put the name of the play and the name of the child to whom it belongs. This small expense is worthwhile. The children are proud of their scripts and the folder helps them keep everything together.

After the children have had the scripts for about a week, we read it together in class. I read aloud while they follow along silently. We discuss the story, who each character is and how he or she would act. We discuss the scenes and any confusing lines. The children may not understand some of the humorous lines, either because of unfamiliar idioms or because of the sarcasm used by the character. This is also the time to talk about the love interest in the play and how it is handled in the script. I inform the children that, if they cannot handle the "mushy" lines, they should not try out for certain parts. The most that I have been able to achieve with children of this age is handholding. One script required the lead characters to dance a waltz together. A lack of experience in ballroom dancing made the children look awkward — all feet. They managed though, and the audience understood. Some children are simply unwilling to try, and they should not audition for a part they cannot handle. When actually rehearsing those scenes in later months, if a child resists hand-holding, for example, I remind him of the commitment made when he auditioned for that part. All children know of the requirements of the various parts from the beginning, and in accepting a part they agree to perform what is required.

The next step is to send home a letter with the children to inform their parents of the audition date and the costume requirements for each part. The leads have greater costume needs than do the lesser parts. Parents have a right to know what costumes will be necessary for particular parts before the children audition.

Included in that letter should be a tentative rehearsal schedule. We hold all dramatic rehearsals after school, and each lasts for 30 to 45 minutes. Longer daily sessions are unproductive. Youngsters are already tired from a full day at school, and many have other activities planned for their free time. No matter how you schedule rehearsals of various scenes, the lead characters are usually required at most if not all of them. Therefore, children who have a heavy after-school schedule of piano or dance lessons or athletic activities are not encouraged to try out for major parts.

One year I had a talented little girl who was heavily committed to various after-school activities. There were times when she even had difficulty keeping up with her school work. Yet her mother encouraged her to try out for the female lead in the play. As her teacher I could see, perhaps better than her mother, that the child would simply be unable to cope with another big undertaking. She was assigned a lesser part. She gave an excellent performance, and the relief that she felt at not receiving a major part was evident in class. She was a much happier youngster than she would have been otherwise, and the decision was not hers. She could save face at home because the *teacher* had not placed her in the lead part. If I had not worked closely with this child in the classroom I would not have known the pressure she was under from other activities, and I might have given her the lead. This would have made an already hectic schedule worse for her. As things turned out, I had a happy child, able to cope with what was expected of her.

Seeing a Professional Show

Another activity which should be mentioned in your mid-November letter to the parents is the possibility of taking interested children to see a professional version of their play before they are

1. *Annie Oakley*
Act I, Scene 1.
Old hat, loose
blouse, old skirt.

2. *Annie Oakley*
Act I. Scene 2.
Cowboy hat, white
blouse, red vest
and skirt, cowboy
boots.

3. *Annie Oakley*
Act II.
White sequined top,
white skirt, red
taffeta sash with
medals, tiara.

4. *Frank Butler*
Cowboy hat, western
shirt, string tie,
trousers tucked into
boots. Optional:
vest.

**This page and opposite: costume suggestions
sent with letter to parents (see page 26).**

**5. *Indian Dancers,
Buffalo Bill* and
*Pawnee Bill***
Buckskin shirt and
pants with fringe.
Indians: feather
headband, barefooted.
Buffalo Bill and
Pawnee Bill: cow-
boy hats and shoes.

**6. *Minnie, Nellie*
and *Jessie***
Simple blouses,
knee-length skirts,
knee sox, shoes.
Optional: pina-
fores.

7. *Jake*
Shirt, collar
turned inside,
suspenders,
knickers, knee
sox, shoes.

8. *Women* and *Girls*
Blouse with high
collar and brooch,
long sleeves (leg-
of-mutton or regular)
skirt (long for
women, short for
girls). OR long dress.

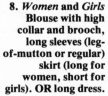

called upon to perform it. Most years we have been fortunate in locating a local dinner theater producing our show. We always charter a bus for the trip. One year when no local group was doing our play, we went to a city 100 miles away, where a theater group was performing it. We had a wonderful time! A dinner theater or community playhouse is usually within the price range of most families.

It is extremely valuable for the children to have an opportunity to see their play done by someone else. They are better able to perform the parts of their characters after watching adults do it. One year we arranged to see a play *before* we held our own auditions. As it turned out, the children did not know whom they were to portray in our play and thus did not know which character to watch. They did not receive as much benefit from this experience as other groups who attended a show *after* our play was cast. So try to schedule such a trip in February or March — the timing is better for the children. One year we could find no group doing our play. The children managed beautifully. Yet, who knows what they might have achieved had they seen another version of their show. The adults responsible for the technical end of the show always gain a lot of ideas from seeing another version also. In addition to new ideas to try out, they often spot problem areas to avoid. It is a valuable experience for everyone when you can arrange it.

Audition Announcement

Your letter to the parents may resemble this one:

> Dear parents,
> The time has arrived at last when we will begin work on *Annie Get Your Gun*. Auditions will be held after school on Wednesday, December 3 and Friday, December 5. The cast will be announced on Monday, December 8. The children will then have until January 5 to learn all of their lines well.
> Rehearsals will begin on January 5 and will be held *each day* for approximately 45 minutes during the months of January through April 9. This show will be truly a team effort and it is essential that each child who has a speaking part be able to participate in scheduled rehearsals. Therefore, we do not encourage a child to try out for a major part unless he has an after-school schedule that will permit attendance at required rehearsals. Every child who is in a particular scene will be expected to stay for rehearsal on the days when his scene is practiced. Please sign and return the enclosed permission slips for auditions and rehearsals.

Each child will have a part in this production, either on stage or behind the scenes. Those who participate in auditions will be guaranteed a speaking part. We also need a stage crew, prompter, and someone to operate the lights.

Enclosed is a detailed account of the costumes suggested for the various parts. If a problem arises in meeting these needs, we will be happy to adapt ideas using available materials. We are flexible because we realize that some fabrics or designs may be hard to find. Please let me know if some difficulty arises.

We would like to take interested fifth graders to see a professional version of *Annie Get Your Gun* before our performance. If you hear of a local dinner theater or drama group that will be presenting the play, please contact me. You might even check with friends in other communities within a 100 mile radius of our town.

We have a very exciting time ahead of us! We wish to thank you in advance for your cooperation.

Sincerely,
Beverly Ross

- -

My child _____ has my permission to attend auditions for *Annie Get Your Gun* after school on December 3 or December 5.

Signed _____

- -

My child _____ has my permission to attend 30–45 minute rehearsals after school during January through mid-April for *Annie Get Your Gun*.

Signed _____

IV

Auditions and Casting

The calendar shows early December. Although you have spent months working on the play, your children have yet to be actively involved. It is now their turn. They are already excited, knowing that you have held a parents' meeting. They have their scripts in hand. As Audition Day approaches, you must explain exactly what will be expected of them. Each child will be required to read a portion of the script, about one-half a page, chosen by you and announced ahead of time. Each will be asked to sing a solo, preferably a song that he knows *well*. As soon as you make that announcement, someone will ask whether he must sing if he is trying out for a non-singing role. My answer has always been yes. I explain that singing shows me two things that I cannot see in any other way: (1) whether or not he can sing and (2) his "stage presence," or how he handles himself on stage. He is likely to be very nervous while he is singing, but if he still does well, he can be counted on to give a good performance in front of an audience. One year a child who tried out for a lesser part did such an outstanding job that she was chosen for the lead. This would not have been possible if she had not sung a solo during auditions.

Prior to auditions I give each child a form to fill out and return to me. I discuss it in detail with them, particularly the last line which says "I (will, will not) accept any speaking part for which I am chosen." I point out that many people are trying out for the same part. A child who is unwilling to accept *any* speaking part severely limits himself. If he is willing to accept any speaking part, he has a much better chance of receiving another good part if it is impossible to give him his first choice. If you have more than 20 children auditioning, schedule two auditions and note each child's assigned date on the Audition Date line. Sometimes one date is more convenient than another for a particular child because of medical appointments, etc. This is the form we use.

TO BE FILLED OUT BY AUDITIONING CHILD.

Audition date: _____

Child's name _____

I am trying out for the part of _____

I am also interested in the parts of _____

_____

I _____ accept any speaking part for which I am chosen.
  (will, will not)

Audition Judges

Which adults participate in auditions and casting? The Director is, of course, the most important person in attendance. As the classroom teacher, she knows the children better than anyone else. She has spent the first three months of the school year mentally storing knowledge about each child, his capabilities and his tractability. She also is well aware of the child's academic situation. When first discussing the play with my class in September or October, I always point out that a major consideration at the time of casting is whether or not a child who is chosen for an important part is able to handle the additional workload of many rehearsals in addition to keeping up with required schoolwork. The child who is lax about turning in class assignments or homework will not receive a major part. This is an added incentive in the classroom to the child who is inclined to be negligent about his homework. Motivation is thus added to the classroom situation.

In addition to the Director, another essential adult at auditions is the musical accompanist. The school music teacher may take part. She has the advantage not only of having musical training, but also of knowing the children. She knows the music she teaches in class and therefore the songs that the children are likely to choose as their solos, and she is able to accompany them.

You need at least three adults participating in auditions. If you are working with another teacher, she is your valuable third. She has been storing information on her students as you have. Her instincts are sharp and can be completely relied upon. If you are working alone, ask a friend to participate. Sometimes a completely objective view from someone who does not know the children outside of what she sees at auditions can be very helpful. You may wish to have as many as five adults present provided they are not parents of students who are auditioning, but even that worked satisfactorily for us one year. Our wonderful Musical Director had a daughter in my class. We needed her expertise in casting our play so she attended auditions. During the casting process when we began evaluating her child, she left the room and took no part in our discussion. Her child was a talented young lady with a lovely singing voice and our decision was relatively easy. She could not be the leading lady because she was several inches taller than our leading man. She was cast in the part of the second female lead. What a superb job she did!

Once the audition panel has been chosen and the dates for auditions set, collect all those forms from the children indicating the parts in which they are interested. Then make a master sheet, compiling all the information for your panel. My master sheet looks like this.

Child's name	First choice	Second choice	Third choice	Part given
Linda	Annie	Dolly		
Todd	Frank	Charlie	Buffalo Bill	
Dean	Frank	Charlie	Buffalo Bill	

When audition day arrives, give each member of the panel a copy of the master sheet and a Speaking and Singing Voice Evaluation sheet so that each will be using the same rating system. Columns are wide enough to enable you to indicate a plus (+), check (✔), or minus (−) and also a few words of comment if necessary.

Child's name	Speaking voice		Singing voice	
	Volume	Expression	Volume	Pitch
Linda	+ loud!	no shyness + excellent	+ great!	+

Audition Day

It is wise to use a large room for auditions—perhaps the school cafeteria. You will be better able to judge the volume of a child's speaking or singing voice if you are some distance from him. The children are told that two things we will be watching for are how loud they are and how slowly they speak. The importance of this will be covered in the chapter on Direction.

For the reading portion of the audition, it is best for you to preselect the parts of the script to be read by the children, generally a conversation between two characters. I choose lines that show drama or express emotion. For lead parts I always choose lines involving the love interest to see how the children will react to this type of pressure. In auditions I ask another adult or an older child such as a past show star to play the scene with every auditioning child. Thus I achieve consistency and fairness. If each child reads with a friend, one partner might read better than another and thereby give the auditioning child an unfair advantage.

In the singing portion of auditions, the one vital element to watch for—something with which you are born—is *pitch*. If a child cannot sing a note played on the piano, there is probably no way anyone will be able to teach him to do so. The child who can usually sing on pitch but has an occasional lapse can usually be taught with practice. Perhaps the best song for showing whether or not a child has good pitch is "America." The note intervals in this song are difficult, and a child whose pitch is not good will have trouble with it. Even the unpracticed ear can hear the incorrectly sung notes. You do not want to place a child in a lead part which requires him to sing if he cannot accurately hit the notes of the songs. Not only would this reflect poorly on the show, but it would also be extremely embarrassing for him. He could perhaps "talk" the words of a song or in a large group of singers he could either sing softly or simply "mouth" the words.

The average fifth grade child has a vocal range of approximately 12 notes, beginning with A below middle C and ranging upward. Any music in a show that has notes outside of this range will present problems and your accompanist may have to transpose the music. So you want to find the children who have the widest ranges. The child should first be asked to sing a scale going as high as he can and then as low as he can. The accompanist should note on her evaluation sheet the notes the child reached at both ends of the scale. Next, the child sings a song that he has selected. The type of song chosen tells something about the child's willingness to work on music in future months. A difficult or a very rhythmical song might indicate that a child really wants a particular part and is willing to work to get it. The child who is not really prepared, who chooses a simple song that has not required effort on his part, indicates he is less willing to spend the time in developing good singing techniques for the show.

Tremendous singing volume in auditions is not terribly important to our Musical Director. As a voice coach, she knows how to build volume in a singing voice. She does not stress that the child already have it in auditions. The only exceptions would be those children who have *no* volume. They are eliminated from singing parts. A low volume can be increased in the months ahead. If you will be working with a musical accompanist and not a voice coach, you must choose children with natural volume for parts that require solos.

Casting the Play

After each child has had the opportunity to conquer his nerves and give his "all" in auditions, your job really begins! After all of the children have been sent home, the panel will meet. Casting the leads comes first. You must consider many things. First and foremost, you must eliminate from consideration those children who have difficulty maintaining an adequate academic record in the classroom. You have told the children you would do this — stick to it! Then you must balance many other considerations. The attitude and the behavior record of the child are most important. Is he able to follow directions? You certainly will be giving many in the coming months. Will he try whatever you suggest? If he is stubborn, you could immeasurably add to your difficulties. Is he a behavior problem in class? A teacher-director cannot give her full attention to a play rehearsal if she must continually discipline children. How tall is he or she? Even in elementary school it will look peculiar if your leading lady towers over your leading man. Girls of this age seem to grow more rapidly than boys. Another major consideration is the child's singing voice. The main characters usually do most of the singing and must be able to sing well. I remember one little boy that we thought would be dynamite in a secondary lead. Yet he had a solo in the show, and he *could not sing!* He was simply tone-deaf! We decided to gamble and hope we could teach him to "talk" his song. He was a sensation! His sparkling eyes and his desire to please conquered all. The audience loved him!

As the panel proceeds down the list of characters in the play, casting becomes easier. Academic considerations weigh less heavily.

For some reason, many plays have a predominance of boys' parts and not too many for girls. We have therefore cast girls in boys' parts. In fact, well before auditions I point out this situation and discuss it with the children. Girls are told to consider seriously trying out for boys' parts. This creates more competition for the boys, and it takes the girls time to adjust to the idea. We have always followed the true sex of the child in casting the male and female leads, but for the rest of the parts we consider the talent of the child rather than his or her sex. In one of our shows a little girl played the part of a prince. When we saw a professional version of our show, it was obvious to all that our "prince" did a much better job in her part than the professional actor who played it in the theater. Boys are unwilling to accept girls' parts, so don't consider that. Besides, you usually have enough parts for boys.

The most essential thing of all in casting is to make each child feel important. Each child who auditioned must receive a speaking part, no matter how small. A child who spoke so softly that you could barely hear him could be given a line that is not essential to the progression of the story. We followed this procedure with a child who had a severe speech problem. He participated in auditions so he earned his speaking part, even though it was a small one.

In addition to the cast, you will need a stage crew. Prior to auditions I ascertain which children are interested in this job. Four youngsters seem to be the right number for this position. They must be very responsible children, for any inattention to detail can slow the tempo of the play. An inappropriate stage setting can be a disaster. Some children simply have no desire to be actors but would love to be on the stage crew. Or, your coed stage crew may be cast members with minor parts if necessary.

You will also need a Lights Technician. Sounds important, doesn't it? This is the only individual in the entire group who cannot appear on the stage. He operates all stage lights and/or spotlights. He must have a script at his fingertips so he can follow the action of a play and turn the lights on and off at the appropriate times. He does not have to attend rehearsals during the first weeks. In March, when we begin to work on the actual stage, he must practice his job just as everyone else does.

Another essential for every play is a prompter. This child must be a good student who reads well. The prompter must be at *every* rehearsal! He is needed for every scene. I always stress the importance of this job before I ask who is interested. You should try, if possible, to choose a person who has no other part in the play. He cannot serve as prompter when he is acting on stage. If you are working with a limited number of children, it may not be possible to have a full time prompter. You may have to choose one from your list of minor characters. In doing so, you have made still another child feel important by adding to his part. One year we did a long play with a small number of children. Each character was on stage many times. I filled my prompter requirements by using *two* prompters. Each was assigned a part of the script for which she was responsible. There was only one part of one scene when both girls appeared on stage at the same time and during that time we managed without a prompter. It was unavoidable but the system worked adequately. There is a solution to every problem if you can only find it.

Each Child Is Important

To make each child feel important I rely heavily on the manner in which I announce the cast. The main characters are never a worry. Their peers know the value of the lead parts, as well as the secondary leads. It is the children with only two to four lines that concern me the most. To build their importance, I make sure their names are listed several places on the cast list. Perhaps I am able to cast a child in two parts, each of whom speak two lines. To me this is as good as casting him in a single part with four lines. I always have a dance production number in my shows, and every single child with a minor part is a member of that dance troupe, as many as 20 to 24 children. I usually have some type of elaborate finale where I again use all those children with minor parts. All dance and finale troupes are listed separately. The key to soothing disappointed feelings on the day the cast is announced is to give a child with a minor part an opportunity to see his name listed as many times as possible. One year I even had one child do a tiny solo right in the middle of the dance number—the word "solo" works miracles!

A few days after auditions are over, announce the cast. The children will be nervous wrecks from the suspense by this time, so do it as soon as possible. We try to hold auditions at the end of the week and announce the cast on Monday. The cast list includes the names of the cast, stage crew, lights technician and prompter. "Announce" is perhaps the wrong word; you surely do not do it orally. Children seem better able to handle the written word than the spoken. It seems to be more private. When my students arrive at school on Monday morning, the cast list is posted at the front of the room. As the children enter they immediately run to look at it and learn what their part is. The disappointments are digested in the confusion and activity that is a part of any classroom on Monday morning. I have never seen tears as a result of a cast list being posted. If a child's part is a minor one, he is able to salvage his pride by seeing his name listed several times. Lead characters have none of these boosts — they do not need them.

Once after the cast list had been posted, I was faced with a new problem. Three little girls, each in turn and each in private, came to me to ask why she was not chosen for the lead. My first thought was to be very careful of what I said since children this age are very sensitive. Yet I couldn't pause before I replied or they might think I was not telling them the truth. I decided that I had to be honest with them while at the same time phrasing my answer so they did not feel rejected. To the first two girls I truthfully said that they had difficulty staying on pitch while singing. I told them that this skill came to different children at different ages. As they grew and matured they might easily develop a more accurate "ear" for pitch and in future years might well be able to do a fine job of singing. Right now, while their speaking voices were loud and expressive, their singing voices just could not handle the demands of the lead part. They both accepted what I said with great understanding. I had allowed them hope that this skill might come later.

The third child had lost the lead part for an entirely different reason, one harder to explain to a ten year old. She had a beautiful singing voice. The reason for her casting was an intangible one, based upon a feeling and observations I had made of her. It was not readily describable. Yet I had to make her understand. The play was *Annie Get Your Gun*. The lead character, Annie Oakley, was an uneducated girl from a rural area in Ohio in the 1880's. She could not even read or write at the beginning of the story. She was an incredible marksman, though socially she had never had any of the usual advantages. The child who was chosen to play Annie was an adorable little pixie with a round face and short, blonde hair. She was a typical ten year old with lots of bounce and sparkle. My questioning child was a taller, beautiful girl with long, dark hair and a more reserved manner. She was more sophisticated in her actions than many girls her age. I tried to answer her by explaining that she was "too classy a lady" for the part of Annie. Had we been doing a play more in keeping with her personal character, she might well have been chosen for the lead. I emphasized her talent and beauty as I talked to her. I am not sure that she understood all of what I was trying to say to her, but she accepted it with good grace. In the part she played, that of the secondary lead, she came across as an elegant — almost regal — lady, exactly the character she was portraying. The audience marveled at her beauty and bearing. She was superb in her part! I truly think that the audition panel, faced with that difficult casting decision, made the right choice on the basis of an intangible "something" that we simply felt was right.

Once the cast is announced, it is *never* changed. I have made a public commitment to each child, and I will not renege on that commitment! As soon as the child reaches home that afternoon with the news to his parents about which part he has, his parents begin to think of costumes. A broken commitment to a child would also be a broken commitment to his parents who may already be making an early investment in costumes and accessories for him. Even if once rehearsals start you find you have made a mistake in casting, you must live with it. Never, never deviate from that first posted cast announcement — unless you enlarge a particular part. That action produces nothing but joy, and you can live with that!

V

Rehearsals

It is now early January. The winter school holiday is over. Your cast has spent its vacation time working on lines. I have tried two systems with children as they memorize lines. The first was that I allowed them to work during this time independent of my direction. When rehearsals began, I found that I frequently had to correct how the children said the lines. They placed different emphasis on words or phrases than an adult would. Once a child has learned a line in a particular way, it is difficult for him to change it. My second system works better although it puts an added burden on me at a particularly busy time of the year. The results seem to warrant the additional time and trouble. During December I set up appointments with all the lead and secondary lead characters and the parents who will be working with them most often on memorizing. At the child's home, we go over his part, line by line, while the parent listens. The child reads each line, and I tell him how it should be spoken. He marks his script, underlining key words and making whatever notations are necessary to help him remember how to say it. The parent listens and remembers also. Thus, when rehearsals begin in January, the child is generally able to deliver his lines in the prescribed fashion, and I have to do less correcting. Rehearsals run smoother with fewer interruptions from the Director.

Scheduling Rehearsals

You will divide the script into sections for rehearsal purposes. Those divisions do not necessarily fall according to scenes. Some scenes are far too long to practice in one session, particularly in the beginning. I try to divide the sections according to cast requirements. Some parts of a scene deal with only a few characters, and other parts with other characters. My divisions are made so that certain children stay after

37

school one day and others another day. It seems wasteful to ask a child
to stay after school to say only a line or two. It is better to continue
rehearsal the day before until the child says his line and then begin a
new section the next day. This is not always possible, but try to do it
whenever you can.

In the beginning the most difficult rehearsals for you are when
the entire cast must attend. In a crowd scene when there are many
people on stage but only a few have lines, the others become restless
and disruptive. It seems easier to require only those with speaking parts
to attend rehearsals during January. Children with non-speaking parts
can be worked in later when you have "polished" the main characters.

Once you have divided the script into sections, notify the
children and have *each* of them mark his script accordingly. Our scripts
usually divide into 10 to 12 sections. After you announce the divisions,
make up a master sheet listing each section and the characters who appear in it. Give a copy to each child. This may seem like wasted effort to
you. After all, each child can easily look at his script to determine
which sections call for his presence at rehearsal. Remember the age of
the child though. They can look, but they don't! So a master list is the
best answer. It makes things easier for the parents too. With the list
and a rehearsal schedule at home and the script at school, a parent is
able to tell at a glance whether or not his child is at rehearsal. Be sure to
post a copy of that list in your classroom. Mine is used by children
every single day. "Do I have rehearsal today?"

Here is a sample portion of my master sheet for *Annie Get Your
Gun*.

Section 1	*Section 2*
Charlie	Frank
Dolly	Wilson
Buffalo Bill	Charlie
Crowd	Mac
	George

Each Friday I announce and post in the classroom the rehearsal
schedule for the following week: Monday–Section 1, Tuesday–Section
2, Wednesday–Section 3, and so forth. No child can give the excuse, "I
didn't know I had rehearsal." In fact, I also write on the chalkboard
daily which section will be rehearsed that day. When the schedule is
announced on Fridays, each child is required to copy it down and take
it home to his parents who will then know which days he will be coming
home late from school. The parents know the schedule for the

following week is announced on Friday and they ask their children for it. It saves much trouble all around!

During January we usually rehearse one section per day. In February we begin to draw together two sections a day, unless one particular one needs extra work, in which case we still tackle it by itself. March is the time to combine several sections a day. This process usually requires more than a 45 minute rehearsal. You can either use the last 30 minutes of the school day as we do, or you can extend rehearsal time from 45 minutes to 75 minutes after school. *Be sure* to notify the parents if your rehearsal times are extended. You are working with young children, and their parents will worry if children do not arrive home at the expected time. *Annie Get Your Gun* was the long play I mentioned. My March letter to the parents and my schedule for final rehearsals went like this.

Dear Parents,
　　March will be the last month of rehearsals and I am able to announce our complete schedule ahead of time. All children should attend all rehearsals from now on. The numbers on the schedule refer to the sections of the play that will be practiced each day.

March 2–March 6
Monday: 5–8 — 3:15–4:00 p.m.
Tuesday: 1–4 — 　　"
Wednesday: 5–8 — 　"
Thursday: 9–12 — 　"
Friday: 13–15 — 　"

March 9–March 13
Monday: 1–6 — 3:15–4:15 p.m.
Tuesday: 7–10 — 　　"
Wednesday: 11–15 — 　"
Thursday: 1–6 — 　　"
Friday: 7–10 — 　　"

March 16–March 20
Monday: 1–10 — 2:00–4:00 p.m.
Tuesday: 11–15 — 　"
Wednesday: 1–10 — 　"
Thursday: 11–15 — 　"
Friday: 1–10 — 　"

March 23–March 27
Monday: 2:00–4:00 p.m.
Tuesday: 　　"
Wednesday: 　"
Thursday: 　"
Friday: 　"

entire play each day

　　Another notice will be sent home near the end of March announcing the Dress Rehearsals and performance schedule and times. All costumes must be finished before the end of March.
　　Thanks for everything! We're going to have a GREAT show!
　　　　　　　　　　　　　　　Sincerely,
　　　　　　　　　　　　　　　Beverly Ross

Your place of rehearsal may be a problem since most schools have limited space available. During January and February I hold rehearsals in my classroom, pushing back the desks to make room. I have marked off the stage size with masking tape on the floor. During March we rehearse on the stage in our school cafeteria-auditorium. It is 11' × 16' × 15" and collapses accordian-style to be stored. It has no curtain at all, either front or back. At the end of a scene, our lights technician turns out the stage lights to indicate scene changes and to allow the stage crew to change sets when necessary.

Our cafeteria-auditorium is small and cannot accommodate a large audience so for our big community performance we move to the stage at the local junior high school. That stage is much larger than the one at the elementary school and has both front and back curtains. The children must learn to spread out on that stage and use overhead microphones. Their entrances and exits and all other mechanics of staging remain the same.

The experience of working on two different stages with entirely different equipment is excellent training for the children and they become quite adept at it. We are usually invited to perform our show for other area schools. Because of their experience with the two vastly different stages, they are able to perform on other unfamiliar stages without any rehearsal or a moment's hesitation. They become versatile little actors and actresses.

Staging

One of the first things to do in rehearsal is to tell the children where to enter and exit, where to stand while on stage and how to move for each section of the play. For some reason children think they must stand still on stage while speaking. They must be taught to move while they talk, but the method of movement is important. Refer to the chapter on Direction for a full discussion of staging a play.

As rehearsals progress you will need stage floor markings. My children always stand too far back on the stage. I put a piece of masking tape across the stage near the front and tell them that they usually will do all of their speaking on or in front of that tape line. We always use tape markings for our dance routines and finale. Without them, a circle dance formation may have a sausage shape instead. If there are overhead microphones, I tape an "X" directly below each on the floor. It is much easier and looks more natural to glance at the floor than to look above your head for the mike.

Entrances and exits require special attention. If a character exits stage left, he must enter from that side the next time, especially if he enters again in the same scene. If your stage has no curtain around the back, behind which the children may walk unseen by the audience, this is especially important. It is possible to cross the stage between scenes when the lights are out, in order to enter from the opposite side, but certainly not during the same scene. My scripts always indicate which side characters enter and exit. The terms "stage left," "stage right," "upstage" and "backstage" all refer to direction as one stands on stage and faces the audience. As long as you are teaching the children about the theater, you might as well use the correct terms.

The Prompter

Your prompter must attend every single rehearsal. This child must practice his craft just as the actors do. Tell him that to be a good prompter he must *never* take his eyes off the script! The instant that he chooses to look up and watch the play action is the time that someone will miss a line. The prompter will have to find his place in his script in order to help the actor. That takes time and causes an awkward pause on stage.

The most important part of a prompter's job is the timing. There is no way you can teach this. You can only help from time to time and wait for the child to develop his own sense of timing. He must not assume too early that an actor has forgotten a line. He must wait just long enough to be sure, and yet not so long that an unnatural pause is created on the stage. He must learn how many words of a line to "feed" the actor before that person remembers the rest of what should be said and continues on his own. In other words, the prompter needs to practice! You must resist the temptation to give him too much help. He must be allowed to develop his skill by himself. By the time opening night rolls around, my prompter usually needs no script—he has unconsciously memorized every line in the entire play! Yet his script is always in his hand, and he still keeps his eyes on every line. Nerves can hit a prompter too, and he just might forget a line at a critical moment and the tempo of the play could be damaged.

Keeping the Fun in Rehearsal

The Director must maintain a high level of enthusiasm during all rehearsals. If you are a classroom teacher, this is difficult after a long day of education, but it is essential for the actors to have enthusiasm and they can get it only from you. Three months of rehearsals can be an eternity to children of this age. It is your job to see that the "fun" never ends. This is easy in January because the children are excited about beginning work on the play.

February can be a long month if you allow it to be. By then the children are beginning to feel they have done their parts so often that they know every line. They could become bored and begin to be sloppy about details. Do not allow this to happen. What is practiced is what will be transmitted to an audience, and boredom or disinterest can also be practiced if you are not careful. This is a time when parents can be a tremendous help. Send a letter home inviting them to attend rehearsal whenever they have the time. A child who has done an excellent job in previous rehearsals may "freeze" when Mom walks in to watch him perform. You may see many nervous gestures that were never there before. If Mom's presence makes him nervous, so much the better. Get that case of nerves over during rehearsals. There will be enough new ones on opening night! An audience of adults, even one or two, relieves the boredom of practice. I do stress that the audience should be parents. I never allow a child's friends to attend rehearsal. Peer pressure produces giggles and silliness and a serious rehearsal is almost impossible. Once in a while, I have allowed a child's *younger* brother or sister to watch but *never* an older sibling. They are too apt to tease a child after rehearsal. Younger ones are impressed, and this is good for the child actor's ego.

Another way to break the monotony of February is to add the musical numbers to the scenes. In January it is better to leave the songs out. Children need to practice those numbers and they do not want to sing even for other cast members until they feel confident. During January soloists practice the songs with the Musical Director or accompanist only. It is best if all music is practiced *before* school. This makes a long day for the children involved, but the songs are usually sung by the leads or secondary leads and these children, extremely dedicated to the play, do not seem to mind. Our children are always willing to participate in before-school music rehearsals. It seems to make them feel more important because they are receiving individual attention. By February they are beginning to know the songs well and are willing to sing in front of other cast members. The first time a child sings in full rehearsal, the cast breaks into applause — what a proud moment for that young soloist! Recognition from one's peers is the sweetest nectar in the world.

In March we move rehearsal to the stage which gives those days the "sparkle" we need. It is exciting to work on a real stage. As they are learning where to stand and how to use the stage effectively, the children realize that they do not yet know all there is to know about this play. They are again interested in learning.

During the routine of practicing, there are many ways to keep fun in the proceedings. Once our leading man was absent from school because of illness, and we had to work around him in rehearsals. I climbed on stage, script in hand, and read his lines in the appropriate places. The children thought it was hilarious. They loved it! When we came to a place where he was to sing a song, the children knew I could not sing, and they were wondering what I was going to do. Well, I mouthed the words while the Musical Director sang offstage. It surely added spice to that rehearsal! We did not accomplish much that day, but the time was not wasted since the attitude of the children received such a boost.

There seems to be one particular line in each play that is adopted by the cast as the "catch phrase" for the year. It's a line that the cast takes as its own, and it is very special to them—an inside joke and a symbol of their working together on such an important project. It is never planned; it just happens. The line is used over and over again in all kinds of everyday situations and always makes the children laugh.

Near the end of March a letter goes home to the parents detailing dates and times of dress rehearsals and performances, and when the children should report for makeup. Permission slips needed for the rest of the activities connected with the show are attached.

Dear Parents,

The great moment is drawing near! Here is a final schedule of show dates and times. Please keep this, and refer to it during the next few weeks. Also, please fill in and return to school the attached set of permission slips. The children may not participate unless we have them.

March 30—2:00 p.m.	Dress Rehearsal at Cedar Park School. Costumes should be brought to school that morning—ON HANGERS! Shoes and accessories should be in a bag attached to the hanger.
March 31—2:00 p.m.	Dress Rehearsal. Pictures will be taken by the cast photographer.
April 1—NO REHEARSAL.	
April 2—8:00 a.m.	Girls and all soloists arrive at school for costuming and makeup.
8:15 a.m.	Boys arrive at school for costuming and makeup.
9:15 a.m.	Performance for students at Cedar Park School.

COMMUNITY PERFORMANCE WEEK

On the days we rehearse at the junior high school, we will leave our school and walk to that school as a group. In case of rain, the mothers on our transportation committee will drive us.

April 6 — 3:00–5:00 p.m.   Rehearse at Westwood Junior High School.
April 7 — 3:00–5:00 p.m.   Rehearse at Westwood.
April 8 — 3:00–5:00 p.m.   Rehearse at Westwood.
April 9 — NO REHEARSAL.
April 10 — 6:30 p.m.   Children arrive at Westwood Junior High School *in costume*, ready for makeup.
    7:30 p.m.   Community Performance.
    9:00 p.m.   (approximately) Cast Party at Cedar Park School cafeteria for all fifth graders and their families.
April 13–17 — SPRING BREAK. (No school, no rehearsals, no performances. RELAX!)
April 20 — 2:00–3:30 p.m. Rehearsal; bring costumes to school on hangers that morning.
April 21 — 8:00 a.m.   Girls arrive at school for costuming and makeup.
    8:15 a.m.   Boys arrive at school for costuming and makeup.
    9:00 a.m.   Bus arrives to drive us to Crestwood Elementary School.
    9:30 a.m.   Performance at Crestwood School.
April 22 — NO REHEARSAL.
April 23 — 8:00 a.m.   Girls arrive at school for costuming and makeup.
    8:15 a.m.   Boys arrive at school for costuming and makeup.
    9:00 a.m.   Bus arrives to drive us to Marshall Hall Elementary School.
    9:30 a.m.   Performance at Marshall Hall School.

This ends four months of work for a wonderful cast of children. I hope they never forget the experience they have had. It has been a pleasure to work with them!

Sincerely,
Beverly Ross

PLEASE FILL OUT THESE PERMISSION SLIPS AND
RETURN THEM TO SCHOOL.

My child, _____ has permission to
walk to Westwood Junior High School for rehearsals on
April 6-9. If it is raining I understand he will ride in a
parent car.

Signed _____

My child, _____ has permission to
participate in the following performances:

    April 10 — at Westwood Junior High School. I will
      furnish transportation.

    April 21 — at Crestwood Elementary School. Trans-
      portation will be by school bus.

    April 23 — at Marshall Hall Elementary School.
      Transportation will be by school bus.

Signed _____

Dress Rehearsal

And so passes March. From here on, excitement is high.
Costumes, props and scenery are added and each builds the momen-
tum. You have been practicing the full play daily for the past week and
are ready for Dress Rehearsal. Actually, the only change in routine is
the addition of costumes and makeup. Find places to hang the
costumes backstage so that each child knows where to look for his. The
children must practice getting in and out of them in the allotted time.
Two dress rehearsals are necessary to work out new problems that
arise. Study the chapter on Performance for a time schedule as well as
other backstage details.

In early April when we are finally ready to perform for an
audience, we put on our show for the students in our school. They
make an excellent first audience. They are not critical of the efforts of
these talented and well-polished young actors. It also gives the children
a chance to become accustomed to an audience before they perform for
the entire community.

Their first performance produces results that will bring tears of joy to your eyes. You are so proud of them! They did it! After this performance we allow for three days of rehearsal on the junior high school stage before our big community performance. If things are going well enough that we need no more practice, the children are given the day off before the big show. If not, I can always schedule another rehearsal.

Expect your Director-nerves to set in. We have spent three months trying to produce the best possible show. Have we succeeded? Our community audience is judge and jury. I know they will like it, but that's not good enough. I want us to knock their eyeballs out!

VI

Direction

Directions to the cast will mean the difference between a mediocre kids' show and a dynamite professional quality show whose actors just happen to be kids. The key to success is the Director's attention to detail. Even the smallest gesture, a smile or a nod, in the right place adds to the overall effect. Children won't think of these things at first; the Director must. So let's get started! Today is the first rehearsal. The children have awaited this moment for three months, and they are filled with excitement. You have chosen your rehearsal area and have marked off the stage dimensions on the floor with masking tape. Tell the children which portion of the "stage" they are to use for exits and entrances. Impress on everyone, especially those who are off-stage waiting to enter, that absolute quiet is necessary backstage. If you set strict behavioral rules on the first day and stick to them, life will be much easier during the next few months.

Blocking Out the Action

On the first day and each day during the next two weeks, your major emphasis will be on "blocking out" the action of the play. This includes such things as where to stand when certain lines are said, the timing for entrances and exits and grouping when there are more than a few people on stage. For some reason, when eight or ten children are on stage, they always stand in a semi-circle, all watching the person talking in the center of the stage. This looks like a chorus line to the audience, and you must continually remind the children to assemble in small groups instead.

"Slow and Loud"

From the first day of rehearsals to the last, I always insist that the children speak in loud voices. They must become accustomed to this method of speaking, and so they are required to do it with every single word spoken. A nervous child who is performing in front of an audience will automatically speak at a faster rate and in a softer tone than normal. Thus, the reverse must become second nature to him, and the only way to achieve that is to do it every single day.

The rate of speaking is as important as the volume. A child must be taught to speak so slowly that when he is nervous in a performance and speaks at a more rapid pace, he is still able to be understood by the audience. I require my children to speak so slowly at first that they feel quite foolish. It becomes a joke to them. I demand to hear not only every word but also every syllable. I stand at the back of the room and insist that they adjust their volume and rate of speech so that I can hear and understand them. I remind them that they will someday be performing in a much larger room than our rehearsal area. "Slow and loud" — those are my by-words!

These two keys — volume and rate — are more frequently commented upon by our audiences than any other feature of our plays. Adults simply cannot believe that young children are capable of a speech delivery that is so easily understood even far back in the audience. At this point in rehearsals I make no allowances for possible future use of microphones. The voices of young children are pitched higher than older children, and this makes them more difficult to understand if they do not compensate for it. With training in volume and rate, beginning with the first day of rehearsal and continuing all the way through with no relaxation of demand, children are able to produce a play where every single line is understood. I have sometimes wished that professional actors took as much care to be understood as do my children!

Eye Contact

Your next rule for children speaking on stage should be: "Face front at all times. Never turn your body farther toward the side of the stage than the corners of the room facing you." Perhaps a professional actor can get away with turning his back to an audience, but a child — NEVER! His voice simply will not carry if he turns too far around. I have a 4″ × 4″ card with a frowning face drawn on it that I insert into the back pocket or belt of a child who habitually turns too far around. When I am able to see the face on the card, the child has positioned himself incorrectly. The child feels rather foolish with this card in his back pocket, and is conscious of keeping it hidden from me by turning his face and body toward the front of the stage.

Another important point to stress is that the child should look at the person to whom he is speaking! This seems like a logical thing to do, and it should not have to be taught. Yet, once a child has memorized his lines, he is inclined to simply stand on stage and recite them. To me this says "Kids' Play," and I am not satisfied with producing a kids' play. I want the children to use professional techniques. So I continually stress to each child that he must look at the person to whom he is talking. The reverse is also true. If someone on stage is talking to him, he must look at that person. To do otherwise would be impolite in society, and you are trying to create realism. Some children, as well as some adults, have trouble making eye contact with another individual. Those children must be directed to give the *illusion* of looking right at the other person. Perhaps he could look at the other person's nose or hairline. The audience will believe that he is looking into the other's eyes.

Directing for Success

Another hint: a child expecting to enter on a particular cue line will usually wait until the other child has finished speaking that line before he enters. This creates "dead" time while the audience waits for the child to walk across the stage to speak. Your entrance cues should be words *in* a sentence, rather than at the end of a sentence. Thus, the child has entered and gone to his proper place before it is his turn to speak, or he could begin speaking as he approaches the others. This must be pointed out to children. In their daily lives they walk and talk at the same time. Yet on stage they won't do this unless directed to.

At most rehearsals you will have no audience or perhaps only a parent or two in February and March. Children must be taught to allow time for audience reaction, even before there is an audience. Point out that they should not say the next line while the audience is still laughing about a previous one. Yet they must not wait until *all* laughter stops. The pause is determined by the amount and volume of audience laughter. The children must develop their own sense of timing in this. I encourage any parent who is watching a rehearsal to respond to script lines in order to help the children perfect their timing.

As children rehearse and learn the lines of other characters as well as their own, they tend to "mouth" the words as others say them aloud. Most do not realize that they do this and will deny it if you point it out. They must make a conscious effort not to be guilty of this for it is *very* distracting to an audience. I remember one child who chronically had this problem. We finally solved it by having him place his tongue lightly behind his upper teeth to remind him to keep his lips still.

Sometimes in rehearsing a script you will find a word or phrase that a particular child will have difficulty saying clearly. I recall a line from one play that gave us trouble. Our ten year old leading man simply could not say "jewelry" so that it was clear to an audience. So "jewelry" was changed to "sparkle," and the problem was solved.

Be aware of hand gestures. Even children who use their hands all the time tend to stand stiffly on stage. They must be told, particularly during early rehearsals, exactly what hand gestures to use and when. Later when they are more relaxed and "feel" their parts to a greater degree, they will include hand gestures without prompting from you. If you do not let them know in the early stages that hand gestures are okay — even preferred — they may not develop others on their own later. Be sure to instruct the children to use their "backstage" hands when gesturing. That is the hand nearest the back of the stage. In using a "front stage" hand, a child may turn his body too far around toward the back and thus may not be heard distinctly. Also, gesturing with a front stage hand draws the audience's eye to the hand rather than to the actor's face. This will not happen if the backstage hand is used.

While we are on the subject of gesturing, you or your Musical Director should instruct the children to use hand motions in songs. A child standing frozen on stage, singing a song, looks most uncomfortable. If a song mentions "sun" have the child make a motion toward the sky; a galloping horse could be indicated by holding invisible reins. Flowers could be symbolized by sweeping the hand toward the ground. If you have difficulty thinking of gestures, go over the song line by line and absorb what the lyrics are trying to say. Then ideas will come to you easily.

So much can be done with the eyes! The adult who knows how to make his eyes "sparkle" adds much to his personality. So it is with children, particularly on stage. This is a skill which must be learned and consciously practiced. Once mastered it may be used whether on or off stage, with excellent results in dealing with others. Open your eyes wide, consciously try to make them bright, and dart them quickly from place to place. This gives a shiny glow over your entire face and denotes a happy individual. Such sparkle from an actor on stage is very distinctive — the audience becomes caught up in his personality. It is particularly charming when it comes from a child actor. Teach this skill to your children, and hope they use it off as well as on the stage. It even helps to create an optimistic mental attitude and makes one a person whose company others enjoy.

Psychology plays an important part in producing a successful play with children. The feelings and ego of the child must be constantly considered. After the first couple of weeks of rehearsals some children will stand out as being exceptionally good in their parts. Their peers recognize this. Those children continue to need encouragement, of course, but not as much as the children who are still weak in their characterizations. If an ego begins to drag, the performance suffers. So praise while correcting those children, and remember to do it in front of the cast. This is contagious, and they will begin to compliment each other. Everyone benefits.

The Love Scene

The love scene in your play deserves special mention because it is a psychologically trying time for the youngsters involved. My cardinal rule is that no child is allowed to laugh at the participants in that scene. I warn everyone that the first penalty for laughing is the culprit will be made to play the scene himself. The penalty for a second offense is to be sent home from rehearsals. This is a disgrace in front of all the others. I have never yet had to use either punishment. Just knowing what will happen is enough to deter laughing!

Naturally, the love scene does not ever involve a kiss. The most that can be expected from children this age is hand-holding. You can do much with this simple gesture to get the idea across to an audience. There is usually a love song involved. My two participants stand at stage center alone. One is singing to the other and looking directly into the eyes of that person. Toward the end of the song the boy takes the girl's backstage hand. Then he takes her other hand during the last line of the song. The effect on the audience as they watch these youngsters is electric — they get the message! If there is no song involved in that part of the scene, the same hand-holding sequence can be performed while the lines are spoken. The eye contact is essential here. Make sure your lead characters are able to look directly into the eyes of another person while talking.

If one of your participants in the love scene has difficulty

The love interest is gently portrayed by hand-holding and eye contact.

speaking a line, tell him to imagine that he is talking not to a classmate but to an adult. He can imagine that he is reciting to his teacher, parent or relative. This suggestion has worked for me. I must confess though that one of our leading ladies simply could not speak a particular line because she was too embarrassed. I considered that line essential to the scene, and I was unwilling to change it. The poor child giggled, turned red in the face, and couldn't even look at her leading man when she said the line. We all dreaded that point in rehearsals because she began to act so silly. By calling her at home after rehearsal whenever we practiced that scene I began to build her confidence. I told her that if she continued in that behavior she would affect the performance of her leading man, as well as draw even more attention to herself and her uncomfortable position. If she treated the situation as normal and spoke the line as though it did not bother her, her peers would accept it as part of the play. I finally convinced her that if she were able to do that line as I instructed, others would simply view it as another part of the script rather than a particularly difficult line.

This advice applies to any child who is secretly embarrassed to recite certain lines. The shy child may feel this way just by having to speak on stage. This feeling in no way diminishes his desire to have a speaking part. Treating his lines as perfectly normal makes his peers accept them in the same way. Children soon begin to accept all lines in a play as coming from the characters in the story rather than from classmates. Audiences accept them in the same way. A frequent comment about our plays from audiences is, "After about ten minutes you forget the actors are children." The self-confidence gained by all the children is incredible. They have accomplished something they never thought possible—performing for many people. Even the child who is normally outgoing and confident feels that he has accomplished something truly remarkable—and he has!

Technical Help

Technical aids are extremely helpful in rehearsals. I always record every rehearsal. Afterwards I listen to the tape and make notes on problems I detect. My tape recorder has a counter which enables me to note the exact place on the tape where something is not right. The next day I go over all my notes with the children, and I am able to play problem portions of the tape for them. Telling a child that he spoke too softly or too rapidly is not nearly as effective as letting him hear himself on a tape. Children are embarrassed to hear themselves on tape especially during early rehearsals and especially when the rest of the cast is listening. This feeling lessens as more and more tapes are played in the following days and weeks. The tape fills another need. It is useful in demonstrating to the child or to the class what a fine job a certain person did in rehearsal. Whether a shy or confident child, he reacts to public praise with even greater effort at the next rehearsal.

As Director you gain much from listening to the tapes. You find lines that have a slightly different emphasis than you would like, and you are able to talk to the child involved so that he can change them. You may *think* that you absorb everything during a rehearsal, but there is so much going on that in truth you miss a great deal. The tape gives you another chance to find errors, and in correcting them you create a more polished show. After you and the children listen to the tape, re-record on that same tape during the next rehearsal. This is an inexpensive though beneficial aid to all concerned.

Creative Problem Solving

As the weeks of rehearsal pass, you will find that the children, even the main characters, have memorized their lines at the beginning of the script much more thoroughly than those toward the middle and the end. If a child is struggling to remember lines, he cannot also keep in mind your many stage directions. It is usually necessary at some point in rehearsals for me to show my displeasure at those who forget lines. Once I "make a scene" the children usually go back to studying their scripts. I tell them that, no matter how well they think they know their parts, it is essential for them to study each night for the next day's rehearsal. I am not sure they do it — certainly not all of them do — but it makes *me* feel better! One can always hope that at least some do take the advice.

Sometimes when a problem arises you simply cannot solve it no matter how hard you try. If this happens, ask a friend to attend rehearsal and give you her impressions or suggestions. The year that we were producing *Annie Get Your Gun* we had what I began to think was an unsolvable problem. In the story there is a shooting contest between Annie Oakley and Frank Butler. The children wore toy guns and holsters, which they would use in this contest. The question was how to make the guns look and sound as if they were being fired at real targets. We tried every system of sound effects that we thought safe and appropriate for use with children. We scoured theatrical supply houses, library books and any other source that occurred to us. I finally decided that whatever we used would simply have to look and sound artificial. A child offstage slapped two small boards together while Annie and Frank fired in the direction of stage right and imitated the recoil of their guns, sometimes with the gunshot sound and sometimes not. A better solution did not seem possible. Then one day our Stage Manager stopped in to watch rehearsal. We happened to be practicing the gun scene with the usual poor results. She suggested changing the way the children stood—so that the audience had a front view of them instead of a side view. From that angle the recoil seemed to match the gunshot sound and everything looked perfectly natural! Such a simple solution! Sometimes "new eyes" can solve a problem that has seemed insurmountable. (See Chapter X under Sound Effects for a full description of this problem as well as how to handle other sound effects.)

As you produce your play you will encounter unique difficulties that I have not. You will solve them the best way you can. Keep in mind that with experience comes expertise. With your first theatrical efforts, your audience will be anticipating something that looks typical of what they expect from that age child. They will be amazed at what you and the children have created! They will rave! Then as the years and the plays go by, your audience will expect more because they know what has been accomplished in the past. You will be ready for the challenge. They expect more and your experience enables you to produce a more polished show each year. Soon you and your children are a true phenomenon, exceeding the expectations of even the most critical audience. The children, hearing the applause and the glowing compliments after the show, feel that they have accomplished something beyond their wildest dreams! The feelings of self-worth and self-confidence developed in all of the children are feelings that every human being ought to be able to experience but many never do. If you ever needed a reward for all your hard work, this is it!

VII

Music

The music is the beauty and the backbone of your show. It will be handled by either of two special people. The first, and probably the easiest to find, is a musical accompanist. The second is a voice coach who can also serve as your accompanist.

Musical Accompanist

Your first play is likely to be handled by a musical accompanist. As soon as you have chosen your script, begin searching for this talented and dedicated gem. While many adults can play the piano skillfully, not all of them will be able to fulfill the demands of this critically important position. The musical accompanist must be willing to give a lot of time to the play. She must be present during every rehearsal beginning in March. Prior to that, you will use a musical tape recording made by her.

For your first show, you will probably find the parent of a cast member to undertake this job. Parents are more likely to be willing to give the necessary time than someone who has no child in the show. If your experience mirrors mine, some of the parents who help with the show will become so caught up in the fun that they will wish to continue working on future shows even though they no longer have a child in the cast. If you are unable to recruit a musical accompanist from your parent pool, put a notice in your school's PTA newsletter detailing that you plan to put on a Broadway musical with your students and that you need an accompanist to participate in rehearsals and performances daily over a six-week period. On the occasional day that she cannot attend rehearsal, you will use the taped music.

The musical accompanist's job is just what the title suggests — playing the piano for a child who is singing. Without the services of a trained voice coach, the child-soloists will purchase a phonograph record of the original Broadway show and learn all of their songs through imitation. The singers on the record are professionals, and the children can learn much from listening to them and trying to sing like them. When the accompanist joins rehearsals during February or March, the child learns to sing the songs with the piano music.

If you will be using only an accompanist, you must find the children who have natural singing volume in auditions. This skill can be taught to children and some of the methods for doing so are described later in this chapter. Your accompanist may not have the time or confidence to teach the children to increase their singing volume and so you must cast children who already have volume in the solo parts.

The most important point to stress to any accompanist is to PLAY SOFTLY! Children's singing voices are not loud by nature. They work hard during three months of rehearsals to obtain more volume. To be overshadowed by the piano is dreadful! Not only will the child feel cheated, but so will the audience who did not come to the show to hear someone play the piano. They came to hear children sing. Have you ever been to a professional theatrical performance where the orchestra obscured the lyrics being sung by the actors? It happens more often than you would expect. *Do not* allow this to happen in your show. Ask the accompanist, "Please play more softly." The more frequently you ask, the sooner she will get the message. Remember to do it the first time you notice a problem. To wait a month for her to notice the situation herself will make your request more awkward. She will wonder why you didn't say something sooner. Save yourself an embarrassing situation and mention it the first day if necessary.

Voice Coach

You may be extremely lucky to find an experienced voice coach among your parents or within the community who is willing to work on your show. This marvelous creature turned up in the parent pool of our first show in the person of Sandy, now our Musical Director. A voice major in college, Sandy is our combination voice coach-musical accompanist. She has worked on every play. Thanks to her talent and dedication, I can completely dismiss from mind all worries about the music for our show. When I have the final script in order, I contact Sandy and tell her which songs we will use. She takes complete charge of all music and does a masterful job year after year.

Sandy has become an authority on how to pull the best musical performance from children. She has developed many tricks over the years, and her expertise will help you to have the best show possible. If you have no vocal coach, perhaps your musical accompanist will be willing to use some of the techniques.

Voice Rehearsals

The play is cast, the winter holiday is over, drama and voice rehearsals begin in January. We hold all voice rehearsals for soloists before school each morning. Arrange a regular rehearsal schedule with the soloists' parents. Find a practice area where there is a piano and privacy. It is best to meet with the male and female leads twice a week at first and always on the same weekday so the children remember to come. Meet with secondary leads once per week.

Lesson 1: Getting Acquainted

Never use the child's given name during a voice rehearsal. Always call him by his name in the play. This helps him to realize that when he steps onto the stage, he ceases to be himself and becomes his play character. By the time you begin working on the love song, you will have already established this difference and you can approach the children with, "Don't be embarrassed to hold her hand. It is not you, the fifth grade child, doing it. It is you, the character in the play."

The child, coming into the first voice rehearsal, wants to start singing, "Right now." Today, though, is get-acquainted day. While the child knows his teacher-Director well, you are someone new who will be telling him what to do in the coming weeks. You do not know each other, and it's hard to trust a stranger. Begin by telling him a little of your musical background so that he will have faith in your knowledge and the things you will teach him. Ask him about himself, his other activities and interests. You must help him to find times when he can practice at home. If he is terribly busy with another activity this month, but things will settle down for him next month, you need to know about it. Be reasonable in your demands. He will appreciate it and will work harder for you.

Now comes the mini-anatomy lesson. The child-singer needs to know something about sound production in the human body. Tell him how the vocal cords work. Use rubber bands to demonstrate. A thin band represents the vocal cords when singing high notes, a medium band for medium notes and a heavy band for low notes. The vocal cords vibrate when a person sings, producing the sound. If you pluck each band in turn, the different tones can be heard.

Tell the child about the vocal selections book and its cost. The children playing the leads need this book. Available at any good music store, it contains the songs for their play. Each soloist must have his own copy since you will be making notations on the music for his use only. Suggest to the child that he listen to the phonograph record of the show to help him learn the melodies and lyrics of his songs. He must learn the songs *before* he begins using his vocal selections book. Does this seem backwards to you? It really is not. The sheet music is not for memorizing purposes. It is for work on diction and breathing. If the child had the vocal selections book, his parent might, with the best of intentions, be tempted to play the songs on a piano at home and teach them to the child incorrectly. It is easier for him to learn a song correctly from his vocal coach in the first place than to have to unlearn one thing and then learn something else.

Ask the child whether he has a tape recorder at home. You will be making a voice lesson on tape for him to use in practice sessions at home. Tell him that he needs to find a time at home when he is *alone*, in which he can practice away from teasing brothers and sisters. If the house is always busy, perhaps he could find a quiet corner of the yard or take a walk and practice while he is walking. The reason for this is that no one, and particularly no child, wants to do poorly when performing in front of others. When he begins to practice new songs, he may have difficulty at first. That is why he needs privacy. The only exception is when the child is working with you, the voice coach. There it is perfectly all right to sound "bad." If he sounded great from the beginning, he would not need you. You are there to help him learn to sound great, so that when others hear him perform, they will be impressed!

To conclude Lesson 1, sing one song from the show for the child. Discuss what the song is trying to say, the purpose for it and the type of attitude with which it should be performed by his character. For example, an exciting song would fall dead if not sung with animation. A cowboy would sing a song in a different style than would a gentle character.

Lesson 2: Diction and Breathing

Back to anatomy: this time explain what a diaphragm is and how it works. Paint a visual picture for the child in describing the diaphragm in relation to the lungs. Tell him to imagine a zipper on the front of his chest. Unzip the zipper and put a blown-up balloon representing his lungs inside; then close the zipper. The diaphragm is the muscle right underneath that balloon. The balloon, when filled with air, pushes the muscle down lower in the body. When the balloon deflates, the muscle raises up to push out the air. This muscle, the diaphragm, is very important in singing because it helps control our breathing. Singers should develop this muscle so that they can let the air out of their lungs slowly and evenly, rather than all at once.

A good way for the child to develop this muscle is to lie flat on his back on a bed with his knees bent and feet flat on the bed. He places a book on the diaphragm, located right underneath the rib cage. Then without moving his shoulders at all, he raises and then lowers the book. Doing this exercise every night before he goes to sleep will strengthen his diaphragm muscle and help him to sing better and with more volume. This exercise should be done while lying down each day for the first month of work. Then encourage the child to try it while standing up, using his hands instead of a book and raising and lowering them by using the diaphragm muscle.

During Lesson 2, begin work on a song. Together you will go through one song in the child's vocal selections book, marking all of the music for two purposes: diction and breathing. Place a check mark in every spot where the child should take a breath. He is always required to breathe at that point, even if he feels he can sing longer without a breath. A nervous child on stage will need more oxygen than one in rehearsal, and breathing points should be more frequent than seem necessary at first.

The diction markings stress certain consonants in words. For a child of this age, the ones that should be stressed by him are l, m, n, t and d. He must be *sure* to pronounce these consonants, particularly when they fall at the beginning or the end of a word. The only stressed vowel sound for a child this young should be the long vowel sound. So in marking his music underline each place where one of the stress consonants appears at the beginning or end of a word. Also, underline all long vowel sounds. Use a red pen so that these points will stand out.

Sometimes, even when a child stresses the proper letters, a word may be difficult to understand when sung. Perhaps that word and the next one sound as if they run together, particularly if the first word ends with the letter "l" or "n." In that case, for diction purposes insert the word "a" in between. For example, to sharpen the sound of "you will stand," have the child sing "you will a stand." Your young singer will think, "That sounds dumb!" Assure him that from the audience "a" will not be heard, because as he becomes accustomed to saying it, he will slide over it, not stressing its pronunciation.

Only one song is studied and marked at each session with the child. That adds emphasis to it and helps his understanding. To cover all of the songs that a lead character must sing will take several sessions, but by meeting with him twice a week, you will soon cover all of them. Once a song has been marked, the child may work on it alone at home. No parent help yet, please!

After his music is marked, you will sing a phrase of the song, and then the child will sing it with you. The child will then sing it alone while you listen. Work out the first phrase in this way, then the second phrase, and then put the two together. Proceed through the entire song in this manner.

Explain to the child the importance of opening his mouth while singing. No matter how much lung power he has, he will produce no volume if the sound can't get out! By holding the first two fingers of his hand together and placing them between his upper and lower front teeth, he will find that this is the best position for achieving the most volume. Of course, some words require that the mouth be closed for pronunciation. You cannot sing the word "need" with an open mouth, but use this skill whenever possible.

A skill that must always be practiced is *breathing evenly*. Instruct the child to wet his fingers and hold them in front of his mouth. Then he is to take a deep breath and let the air out *evenly*. The dampness will enable him to feel the air flow over his fingers. Another excellent exercise to encourage even breathing is done with a lighted candle. For the children's safety, mention this technique to the *parents only*. Most parents are willing to supervise such activity at home. The lighted candle trick is done by placing a candle in a sturdy holder and lighting it. The singer places himself in front of the candle, fills his lungs with air and exhales. The object is to exhale slowly enough so that the candle flame merely flickers but does not go out. Keep the flame moving until the lungs are out of air. This teaches excellent breath control, but it must be practiced under adult supervision.

Lesson 3: Volume and Range

At the beginning of this lesson, explain the necessity for warm-ups. Draw a parallel to athletes who always limber up their muscles before practice or a game to prevent injury. The same is true of singers. You have only one set of vocal cords — take good care of them!

Warm-ups, or vocalizing, consist of singing five notes in

succession with the piano and using the words "lah," "lay," or "lee" in turn. Sing "lah-lah-lah-lah-lah," up the scale and then back down. Then the child begins a half-note higher and goes through the same process again, up five notes and then down five notes. Continue this procedure until the child has gone as high as he can sing. Next he begins at that top note and sings down the scale for five notes and then back up to the starting note. Then he begins a half-step lower and does the same thing—down and up. He continues until he has sung as low as he can. Keep track on a chart of the date and the note range (the highest and lowest notes sung). As his singing range increases day by day, the child will be amazed that he is singing higher and lower than ever before. Here are results in black and white. He begins to see that you really know what you are doing. This will reinforce his trust in your advice and he will be willing to try whatever you suggest from now on.

During warmups pull out your mirror and ask the child to watch his mouth in it. He must always open his mouth wide enough when singing "lah" to insert those two fingers between his teeth. When singing "lee," he must always produce a smile. From now on, a mirror is an essential part of his equipment, as important as his music. Whenever he is practicing at home, he must sing in front of a mirror—either one in his bedroom or a small one if he is out walking. With this one lesson you are teaching techniques for obtaining volume and range in singing. Vocalizing must precede every rehearsal and performance from now on. This is very important!

Never allow the child to sit during a voice rehearsal. Posture is extremely important in singing. The child must stand straight, shoulders back. In these early rehearsals, his hands must be clasped behind his back. When practicing at home after a long day at school, if the child is tired and feels he must sit for practice, tell him to sit on the edge of a chair, his back not touching the chair, his shoulders back and hands clasped behind him.

One of the best tricks for increasing volume is a method by which you have the child focus his tone in singing. Draw a large "X" on a chart and place it as far from the child as possible in the room where you are working. Have him focus on that "X" and sing directly to it. Every word of every song must "hit" the center of that "X". You may not hear the results of this exercise for weeks. If you tape record a child's singing during one of the first lessons and then make another tape several weeks later, the improvement will be quite evident. The volume of the child's singing voice will be greatly increased. The "X" represents the audience although the child does not realize it.

There was one child who developed excellent singing volume

through the use of these techniques. In the beginning she always seemed to lose volume during a song. When that occurred, she was told to omit the words of the song and just sing "lah" for a phrase or two and then go back to the words. By the time our performances were held, she was able to sustain the volume through her entire song. This was a big hurdle for her, and she felt very proud of her accomplishment! So did we!

For this and subsequent lessons, continue to mark the music of one song per day until you have covered all of them. Review the songs previously marked which the child has been practicing at home.

Voice Lesson Tape

By the end of the first month, the child will have learned his music but must continue to practice using the techniques for diction and volume which you have taught him. The parent may now help the child at home, if there is a piano available. If the child hears the parent play something in a different way from what you have taught him, he will recognize it and be able to correct it.

February is the time for the voice lesson tape. Make up an individual tape for each child. One child's tape may contain the following. "Hi, (character name). It's time for your lesson. First let's go through your warm-ups." Play the piano for the child to do his vocalizing. "Now, let's work on (name of first song) ." Discuss briefly the problems that the child is having with this particular song and how to handle them. Play the notes the child will sing for the whole song. Then give the child the dialogue cue line that comes right before the song. After the cue, play the accompaniment, which may vary from the notes to be sung, and you sing the song. Then play the accompaniment so that the child can sing with the tape. Repeat the accompaniment so that the child may sing the song twice. Then move to the next song, listing problems and remedies, playing the notes to be sung. Go through every song that the child sings in the show in this way. The child is expected to use this tape at least three times a week at home. It is even better if he can find the time to use it daily. After the last performance of the show, ask the child to return it to you so you can use it to record a lesson for someone else next year.

The child is not left entirely to his own devices. You still meet with him twice a week. The lessons are shorter now, usually lasting 20 minutes. That means you can work with two children each morning. At this time let the child designate some of the material for the vocal lesson. By this time he knows where he is having trouble, and he will suggest something he feels he needs help on. Of course, you may have spotted a problem area and you will go over that in the lesson too. In early February he will be singing his songs in regular drama rehearsals.

Some songs require a duet, trio or quartet. Perhaps one child sings a line or two and then others sing a line. February is the time to bring those children, who have been practicing separately, together in a vocal rehearsal. Ask them to come to practice at the same time. In one of our shows, a song required four singers, each singing a different melody at the same time, similar to barbershop harmony. Children this age are usually able to handle two part harmony, three part once in a while with lots of work, but four part harmony—never. So what were we to do? Sandy found the solution by using four children but only three musical parts. One child sang the top part, another sang the bottom and the other two sang the middle part. It worked beautifully and the audience could not detect that the harmony was three part instead of four. The quartet created a sensation in the show!

Gestures and Staging for Songs

This is a good time to work on gestures and staging for the songs. To give the child some idea of what to do with his hands, you will have to present ideas to him. Later on he may be able to think of some on his own. Without gestures he will look uncomfortable on stage. The lyrics of the songs will suggest appropriate hand gestures. For example, if the song is about musical instruments, the child might pantomime the motions of playing the instrument mentioned.

Staging a song simply means teaching the child how to move while singing. He cannot stand like a statue in one place. Just as in dramatic rehearsal, he must be taught to move around, taking a step or two in different directions or singing one line to one person and another line to someone else. He should look directly at the person to whom he is singing and that person should look at him. He should remember to make his eyes sparkle, except in a sad song which you will rarely have in a show for children. Smiling while singing is so important! Children can charm an audience as much with a smile as with a beautiful voice. Everyone loves a happy face.

The love song requires delicate handling. Your leading lady and man will be uncomfortable doing this number because of their ages. In this song, the two should sing to each other, stage center. As the next to last phrase is sung, the two should join backstage hands. Then during the last phrase, they join front stage hands, looking right into each other's eyes. When done correctly, these simple gestures create exactly the right mood and achieve the same effect as a kiss between adult singers at the end of such a song.

Musical Ups and Downs

Pitch is the single most important element you watch for in auditions. Some children simply cannot sing, and it would be cruel to force them into a singing solo. Yet I remember one little boy who stood out in auditions as being perfect for a particular part in all respects except one. His sparkling eyes and sunny personality typified the character in the play, yet Jordie was tone deaf. He could not hit a single note that was played on the piano, much less sing a song. Unfortunately, his part called for a solo. We counted on our Musical Director's ability to work miracles, though we knew she would never be able to teach him to sing on pitch. The song he had to perform was very rhythmical with a strong beat. We thought he might be able to "talk" the song instead of sing it. This is difficult for children. They tend to follow precisely the rhythm of the accompaniment. Sometimes during rehearsal Jordie would begin to sing which was disastrous! Sandy finally taught him to talk the words in time to the music as though he were telling a story. When performance time finally arrived Jordie and his song were a huge hit! He talked, rolled those big blue eyes and carried off his number superbly.

In another show we had the same problem with another child who had a two-line solo in a number performed by a large group of children. We taught Larry to "talk" his part too. All was going well until we did the show at another school. During the performance we discovered that Larry's position on stage in that number placed him directly in front of a microphone. We had counted on the rest of the singers to drown him out during the rest of the song. The microphone made Larry's voice heard above all the others! Quick, a solution! We could not move Larry or the microphone so we whispered to him to "mouth" the words instead of sing them. All was well.

Then there was the time when our leading lady came down with a cold just before our evening performance for the community. Her speaking voice, though nasal, could be heard by the audience with the help of the microphones. Her singing voice was another matter. The viruses had outwitted us and we had no solution. We just cautioned her to be certain to stand at the mike location for her three solos. The audience knew she was having difficulty but they understood. Audiences are sympathetic where children's unsolvable problems are concerned.

Once we had a girl who was cast in a secondary lead. Amy had a beautiful voice, yet the script did not call for her to sing at all. We felt that she should have an opportunity to use that fine voice. We went back to the original script, found a song for her that had been omitted in shortening and put it back into the show. It added only about two minutes to the total length of the show, and it was worth it to show off Amy's voice. Another script included a song for a secondary lead. The child who played that part had a beautiful voice, but when she became nervous she lost most of her volume, despite Sandy's exercises. Solution: Make the song a duet by matching her with another girl.

If you look hard enough, you can usually find a solution to almost any problem in a show, whether it has to do with music, drama or staging. Children are versatile little creatures, and they are usually willing to at least try what you suggest. They know that you will demand of them nothing that will make them look foolish. You always do your best to live up to the trust they have in you.

The Overture

Every show needs an overture. It marks the beginning and quiets the audience for the performance to begin. The overture is composed of part of most songs in the show. If you are not using all the songs written for the show, you may not wish to use the original overture. You must arrange your own.

Choose the most important, best-known song in the show for the opening and closing sections of the overture. In between those place the choruses of other songs. Analyze the songs and in what keys they are written. Never place two songs side by side if they are written in the same key. The overture is uninteresting if all the music is in the same key. In addition to key consideration, look at the tempo of the songs. Do not group all fast songs and all slow songs together. Alternate a fast one with a slow one. If you do not wish to use the entire chorus of each song, choose only the parts you prefer. You will need at least four to eight measures of each, however. Examine the notes at the end of one song and choose the next, in a different key and tempo, that will be easy to slide into. You are simply modulating your keys as you go through the overture.

For the evening performance you will have about a five-minute overture. Begin three minutes before show time so that any of the audience not yet in their seats have time to be seated. Then the overture extends two minutes into show time, so that everyone becomes quiet and ready for the show to begin. The curtain opens, and the children are on their own!

When we take our show to other schools, our overture starts as the last few groups of students file in to take their seats. The music quiets the audience, and the show can begin on time. This procedure usually requires a longer overture. You may decide to repeat the entire musical arrangement or you may prepare an entirely different overture that lasts longer. You main object is to quiet the audience and set the mood for the show. Then it's curtain time!

VIII

Dance, Finale, and Encore

Dance numbers are another facet on your jewel, the show. Imagine the shining faces of your young performers, the swirling colors of their costumes, the vitality of their bodies as they confidently move to the rhythms of the music. At the end of the show, the dancers execute a few of their steps across the stage and are joined by the full cast, marching and singing. All of the elements of your show build to a visual and musical crescendo, making an unsurpassed finale guaranteed to bring your audience to its feet. The finale is what your audience will remember; make it smashing!

If the thought of choreographing a dance gives you a big headache, don't despair. It is not as hard as it seems. Easing the chore is the fact that the steps must be simple because they will be performed by children, most of whom have no experience in dancing. Planning a dance is well worth the effort since forming a dance group is a great way of amplifying the roles of your minor characters. I usually have at least one dance number in every play plus a big finale with dancing and singing.

Choreographing the Dance

Reduced to its lowest common denominator, a dance occurs when the dancers enter the stage, move around it in an entertaining fashion so that each approaches the front about the same number of times, and then they exit. At the same time, the dance advances the story a bit and enhances the mood of the show. That statement would put gray hair on the heads of real dancers but the formula works with children.

Perhaps you'll be lucky enough to find a dancer among your parents. For several years I had one set of parents who were quite good at working up simple dance steps in time to the music and teaching them to the children at their home on Saturday mornings, and finally on stage at evening rehearsals. Such dedication on the part of these wonderful people! If you are blessed with such volunteers, take advantage of it.

Usually, however, when you ask for a volunteer to choreograph a dance, most parents head for the nearest exit, frightened of undertaking such a task. You stand a better chance of finding someone willing to *help* you teach the children a dance which is already planned. If that parent has had some previous experience in dancing, the two of you may be able to work together, revising your routine and perfecting it for the children.

To begin, examine your show to see where a dance might fit as an integral part of your story. Some stories offer obvious opportunities in the form of a ceremony, a wedding or a party with the music built in. In other shows you may wish to plan the dance around a song to which lyrics are normally sung. Singing child-dancers quickly become winded. To avoid the sight of your dancers with their tongues hanging out, don't require them to sing as well as dance. Also, limit the dance to a *maximum* of three minutes duration. Consider the possibility of highlighting a solo dancer to add a little spice. A solo drummer, if appropriate, is a tremendous help in maintaining rhythm.

Think about the finale, too, which is different from the dance. While it may incorporate some of the same style and dance steps, it is shorter, and its purpose is to present the cast to the audience for the bows. It will culminate with the full cast facing the audience and singing the closing song in a final rousing finish.

The greatest limiting factor to the number of dancers in the group will be the size of your stage. It's hard to be graceful while bumping into another dancer. Our borrowed stage at the junior high school is 25 × 16 feet and accommodates twenty-four dancers easily. A group of any size from three on up may be used. Simple props such as ruffled umbrellas can be used effectively to add interest to the dance. Allow plenty of room for such props between dancers.

Then consider the style of dance. This is, of course, determined by the show. Your dance does not have to be 100% authentic in its style. It has only to be sufficiently representative in music, movement, and costume to create the proper flavor. That flavor will already be partially established by the story that has gone on before. The audience's imagination will already be on the right track and what your dance lacks in total authenticity will be filled in by that imagination. For example, in the closing scene of Meredith Willson's *The Music Man*,

the town's children must come on stage as a marching band. If you don't happen to have seventy-six trombones handy, you can create the impression of a marching band by dressing your children in bright red band uniforms and big smiles, and having them march on stage in band formation while belting out *Seventy-six Trombones*. No one will miss the instruments. The uniforms and singing will completely carry the moment.

The style of the dance will probably fall into one of the following categories:

- ► Western square or circle dance
- ► American Indian dance
- ► Oriental dance
- ► Ballroom dance
- ► Folk dance
- ► Acrobatic, gymnastic, modern style dance

If you are uncertain about precise style, make another trip to the library for books on dances. Check out performances of local dance troupes such as Indian scout groups, Middle Eastern dance groups, etc. Dancers on TV may give you ideas.

Dance Patterns

No matter what style, our dances are built around a few basic patterns used to guide the many pairs of feet through the dance. These include circles, lines, figure-eights, cross-overs, etc. You, too, can create a dance by combining these basic patterns so that they flow into each other to the tempo of the music. Mix in the flavor and style of your particular dance by altering the way the steps are performed and you have your dance. Presto! Be sure to include a freeze-pause near the end of the dance so that the dancers may accept their well-earned applause before dancing off stage.

Plot your dance on paper. It may resemble the football coach's secret weapon for the all-important Sunday game, with circles and arrows and lots of numbers, but it will help you tremendously to visualize your plan. Then give your dance a test run by rounding up a few adults who are good sports and trying it out. A slight adjustment here and there and you will feel you have produced a pretty good dance for your children. *(Text continues on page 77.)*

Opposite: The *Annie Get Your Gun* cast presents a rousing musical finish.

Dance Patterns (pages 72-76)

KEY

Stage right dancers **X**
Stage right line leaders **⊗**
Stage left dancers **o**
Stage left line leaders **◎**
Leading characters **⊛**
Secondary characters **✱**
Others (non-dancers, non-leads) **+**

Entrances (Reverse for exit)

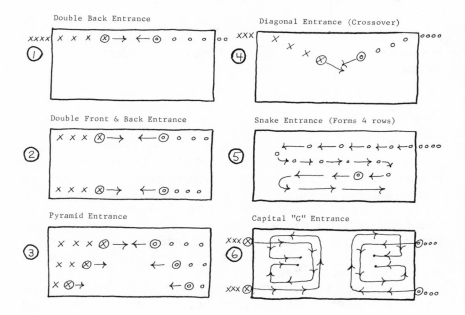

Double Back Entrance

Diagonal Entrance (Crossover)

Double Front & Back Entrance

Snake Entrance (Forms 4 rows)

Pyramid Entrance

Capital "G" Entrance

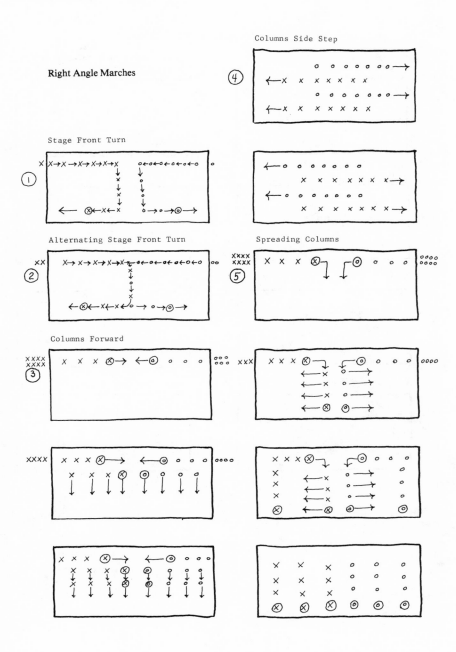

Right Angle Marches

Columns Side Step

Stage Front Turn

Alternating Stage Front Turn

Spreading Columns

Columns Forward

Circle Steps

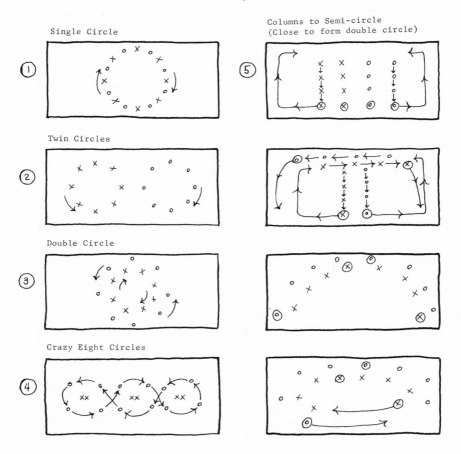

Pairs Patterns

Box Step
(Step one, feet together)

④

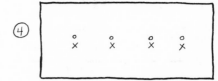

Virginia Reel Pairs

Boy-girl pairs join hands to form arch. Back-stage pair dance through arch to front and join hands to form arch. Each new backstage couple does the same.

①

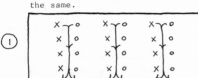

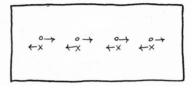

Carousel Step

Boy-girl partners. Boy kneels on one knee, holds girl's hand over his head. She walks around him. Reverse.

②

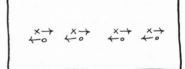

Pair Twirl Step

Boy-girl partners hold hands and swing around, facing each other.

③

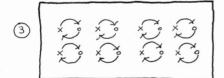

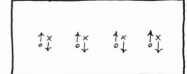

Crossover Steps
(Alternating crossover)

Column Reverse Steps

Hairpin Turn Step
Columns first file front-back-front.
Then front-to-back columns become
side-to-side columns and follow side-
to-side path.

Diagonal Crossovers

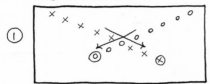

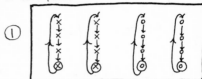

Double Diagonal Crossovers

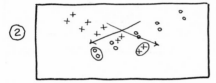

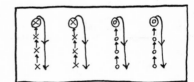

Figure Eight Crossovers

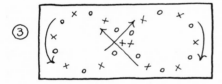

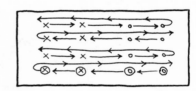

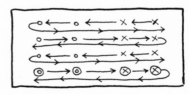

It is best to stay flexible and open-minded at this point. Sometimes what looks good on paper and with adult dancers may fall apart when children try it. Also, what is artistic and appealing from the bird's eye view may be a disaster as seen from the audience's position. So while you will try to work out as many problems as possible before the dance is presented to the children, there will always be minor changes once you begin to teach the dance. The illustration here shows you some simple, basic patterns which you can use to choreograph your dance.

Teaching Children to Dance

There is a simple technique to teaching a dance to children, some of whom haven't a rhythmic cell in their entire bodies. It can be done. The trick is to break the dance down into small parts.

Use no music until the entire dance has been learned. At your first dance rehearsal, line up the children and teach them the basic step of the dance. Even in a simple march, the idea of starting with the right foot may be hard for some children. There are several ways you can help a child who has two left feet. Begin by telling him, "You can do it!" Give a child a challenge and he will rise to it. Then stand next to him and keep trying, or place him in between two confident dancers and ask him to imitate them. The same confusion can occur with hands. I remember a girl who could not instantaneously distinguish between her right and left hands. She was doing a grand-right-and-left routine in a square dance, and she had no time to think. She always stuck out the wrong hand! Solution: she put a bracelet on the hand she was to extend to her partner, and all was well. Practice and practice and practice until it becomes second nature.

Once the feet know exactly what to do, then and only then can you begin to teach the dance patterns. A strip of masking tape stuck to the floor down the center of the stage may help the dancers orient themselves.

(1) Position all dancers on stage in places you wish them to be when the dance begins. Take into consideration height of dancers and spacing between them. Certain dancers will be designated "Line Leaders." They will be responsible for leading their groups onto the stage and through the dance. They should be your most reliable students with a good sense of rhythm and timing. They must listen for cues and start out on the right foot.

(2) Then have the dancers file off stage, keeping in line, to their pre-dance locations in the wings. Have each dancer carefully note his lineup position, and make a list for yourself.

(3) Then have the children come back on stage and teach them the first two or three steps of the routine. Repeat the steps several times that day.

(4) At the next rehearsal, review the lineup and the steps learned at the first rehearsal, and then teach the next two or three steps. Practice all of the steps.

(5) The next time, review all the steps, teach the last two or three, and then rehearse the whole dance.

If one or two dancers are having difficulty, do not embarrass them by singling them out at rehearsal. Either work with them after class or line up the whole row of dancers and have each one go through the troublesome step.

You may wish for a simple technique which will enable you to see how the groups intertwine and whether they are balanced on stage. For example, if your dancers are divided into four groups and each group is wearing a different color, you will want to be certain that the colors are moving in a balanced fashion across the stage. You can do this easily by having each child hold a large sheet of construction paper matching his group's color. That way, long before costumes are made, you can stand back and note that the reds and greens and yellows and blues are well positioned on stage.

On the day you finally add music to the dance, do not expect things to run smoothly. You will need a patient accompanist, since you may find that your dance does not quite fit the music. Work with the dancers and accompanist, adding or subtracting music until it all comes out right.

Once that is done, continue refreshing your dancers' memories by practicing frequently. The first time you add that number to the show rehearsal, around March 1, allow extra time. You will need it.

About two weeks after the children have mastered the dance, they and the rest of the cast should be ready to absorb a new routine, the finale. Teach the finale in the same way as the dance, step by step, but do it during drama rehearsal since it involves the entire cast.

Sample Dance

To demonstrate how the patterns, style and diagrams can be blended for a specific show, consider a dance for Rodgers and

Hammerstein's *Oklahoma!* (see illustration). Naturally, the cast will be belting out a rousing rendition of the title song. The perfect choice for a dance style is square dancing, as popular in the early part of this century as it is now. Even simpler for children is a round dance formation using some square dancing steps.

(1) At the sound of the first notes, two lines of children enter from the back corners of the stage, one from the right, and one from the left.

(2) They move toward the center back of the stage, then forward and around until they have formed two circles. They are holding hands in a chain fashion as they enter. When the circles are formed, each will circle left for several measures of music; then circle right for several measures.

(3) Children then stop and face each other in partners around each circle.

(4) Each child in partnership extends right hand, takes his partner's right hand, and proceeds to "Grand Right and Left" around the circle, using right hand, left hand, right hand, etc. (4a)

(5) When the child is back to his original partner, partners join hands and skip around the circle.

(6) When all partners reach their original places, all children join hands and move to the center of the circle, hands up.

(7) Then they move back to their original places, lowering hands.

(8) Next the child who led the right line on stage originally now leads the circle across the back of the stage and around until a line is formed across the front of the stage.

(9) The other circle on stage does the same routine, but its line goes in the reverse direction, ending up in the back of the first line.

(10) Now you have two lines across the stage, one in front of the other.

(11) Have each line move, side-step, in one direction. The front line moves right, and the back line moves left, for four steps.

(12) Then the lines reverse direction for four steps until both are back in their original position.

Finale and Encore

At this point the dance could easily become the finale number in one of two ways.

Oklahoma! (pages 80, 82–83)

KEY

Stage right dancers **x**   Stage left line leaders ⊙
Stage right line leaders ⊗   Leading characters ⊗
Stage left dancers **o**   Secondary characters **✳**
           Others (non-dancers, non-leads **+**

Dance (24 dancers)

Stage front

Line leaders path indicated.

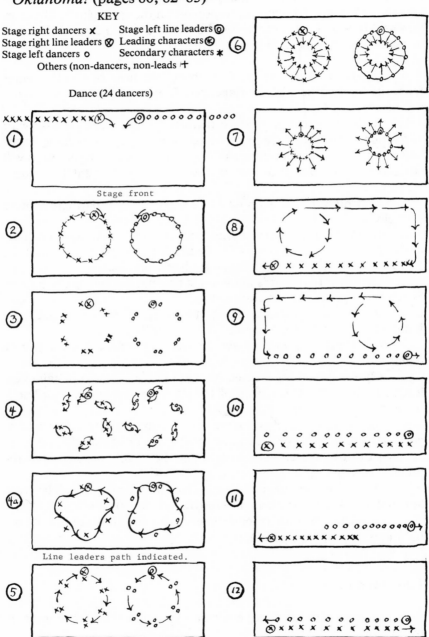

First, see illustration on page 82, "finale A":

(1) The children with lead parts who are not dancers have been standing to the side fronts of the stage, singing and clapping in time to the music.

(2) They now move into place, in a line in front of the two dancing lines.

(3) They should stand with the leading lady and the leading man in the center of the stage, the secondary leads on either side of them, and so on in descending order of importance of parts. They finish singing the song with the entire cast on stage.

(4) Non-dancers and non-leads will form a line behind the dancers. At the last note and shout of "Oklahoma! Okay!" the entire cast raises right arm.

Now see "finale B":

(1) The two rows of dancers split in the center by taking two side steps toward their respective sides of the stage, forming a center aisle.

(2) The leads enter the stage from the back and walk up the aisle toward the audience in ascending order of importance.

(3) They will alternately turn right or left at stage front, forming a line in front of the dancers, with the leading lady and leading man in the center.

(4) Non-dancers and non-leads will line up behind the dancers. The final note is sung and right arms shoot up in unison. Applause!

After the thunderous applause dies down, you must be prepared to go into an encore. Encores don't just happen; actors are prepared for them, so you must teach the children what to do. Here's how (see illustration of *Oklahoma!* encore):

(1) As the first musical notes are heard, the leading actors and actresses in the front row and other non-dancers in the back row will quickly move to their respective sides of the stage.

(2) As the singing begins again, the front row of dancers turns and goes to the right of the stage while the second row goes to the left.

(3) Both rows turn at the side curtain and proceed to the back of the stage. They turn again toward the center and once again form two lines, but this time the second row will be in front and the first row in the back. This will make the parents of row 2 dancers very happy.

(4) Both rows move toward the front of the stage.

(5) The leading characters move back on in their positions for bows as the song ends again. Now bask in the warmth of the applause and get ready for your well-earned bows.

Finale A   Finale B

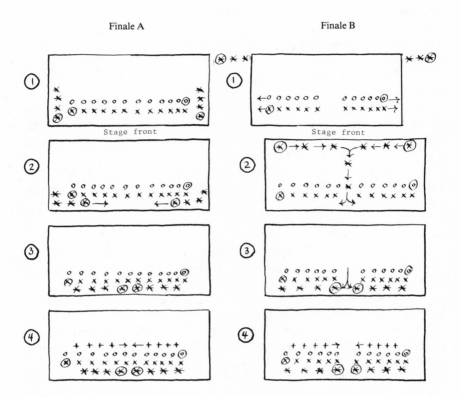

Encore

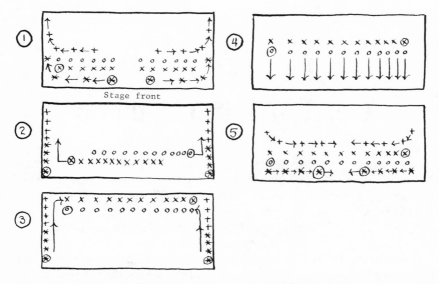

Opposite and above: *Oklahoma!* **(Encore and Finale Dance Steps, see KEY on page 80).**

For our shows we try to have a rousing opening scene, usually with a song. We like to end the same way—with a smashing, ear-jingling song, accompanied by some type of colorful dance or marching routine. Your audience is always left with a particular impression of the show, and all other feelings seem to pale beside the one they experience at the finale. Capitalize on that fact, and do your best to involve the entire cast in an outstanding closing number. It's good theater and you above all are striving for a smash hit!

IX

Costumes and Makeup

Begin work on your costumes *early*, as soon as the winter holidays are over. That allows three months to prepare for an April performance. Our children are responsible for supplying and paying for their own costumes. Their parents are quite willing to assume these costs and this arrangement enables the children to keep the costumes as souvenirs after the show is over.

If a child's costume is unique to the character he is playing, then it is created entirely by the child and his family. We do not become involved other than to suggest the basic design of it based on our knowledge of the show and its time period. A general description of costumes is an important part of the audition announcement sent home in the fall. If the costume must exactly match others in fabric and pattern, then the fabric is purchased in bulk and the costumes are cut from master patterns. The parent pays for the fabric and each sews her child's costume herself. Occasionally after the show families will generously choose to donate the outfit to the Costume Closet for the benefit of future casts.

Costume Coordinator

Jo Ann, our Costume Coordinator, begins planning for costumes during September and October. She checks pattern catalogs at fabric stores, particularly the costume section at the back of the book, to locate patterns that can be adapted for our use. She notes pattern numbers so that she can pass this information on to parents. When identical outfits must be made for a group of children, she purchases the pattern in the size most common to our children, from which master patterns can be traced. Jo Ann chairs the Costume Committee, pairing sewing volunteers with non-sewing parents so that each child is handsomely decked out in time for the show. She works closely with the Director on the many details.

One practical reason to begin work on costumes early is to avoid the pitfalls of seasonal fabric. The perfect fabric you found in October may no longer be available when you get around to purchasing it in late February. If it has to be ordered, it could take many weeks if it is available at all. In our production of *Annie Get Your Gun*, our 19 Indian dancers wore outfits made of a rust-colored velour which looked like buckskin but was much cheaper than the real thing. According to our plan, each child would pay for his own costume, but in order for fabric of each to match, we decided to purchase it all at one time on the bolt. I computed the cost and notified the parents who then sent in the money. When we went to the store in mid-February to purchase the fabric, we found that we had waited too long. Velour is a winter fabric. Stores were selling out and not ordering more. While they still had short pieces of velour, none seemed to have 56 yards in the color we needed. The large *amount* we needed caused the problem. Eventually we were able to purchase the fabric, but we could have saved ourselves much worry if we had attended to it earlier. You have now learned an important lesson from our mistake.

Keeping Costs Down

Cost plays as important a consideration as design in costuming our young cast. Remember that these are children, not professional actors. Their parents are willing to spend reasonable amounts of money on costumes and fabric, but an excess amount is understandably frowned upon. Also, be conscious of the number of costume changes, each of which will add to the total cost. Parents are happiest when stage clothing can be put to a practical use after the show. Minor characters in our play usually wear the same basic outfits for the entire play. The exception is specialty numbers like the Indian dance in *Annie Get Your Gun* when our cowboys and ladies doubled as Indian dancers. In that show our girls with minor parts were dressed in long skirts and high-necked blouses for most of the play. The skirts could be cut off later and combined with the blouses to make pretty school ensembles. The boys with minor parts wore regular pants and either cowboy shirts or dress shirts with collars instead of crew or turtle necks. We added string ties and straw hats or cowboy hats to a few boys for stage interest. All of the outfits were practical, everyday clothing that could be used later so the parents did not object to purchasing fabric for the Indian costumes, even though their future use was probably limited to pajamas or Halloween costumes.

Costumes for the main characters always seem to be an entirely different matter than those for the rest of the cast. Our lead characters usually need two or three apparel changes. Parents of lead and secondary lead characters are willing to spend more money on costumes than those whose children have minor parts. No matter how I consider cost, these parents are always willing to go beyond the call of duty in providing their children with wonderfully lavish regalia. Of course, these extravagant duds emphasize the importance of the main characters and add immeasurably to the success of the show. The mother of our leading man in *Annie Get Your Gun* made him a white satin cowboy shirt with six-inch fringe attached to the front and back yokes. She then made a reversible vest, black velvet on one side and red satin on the other. By adding his vest and then turning it inside out between scenes, he could totally change the look of his costume. She purchased a pair of black pants and black cowboy boots to complete his outfit. She topped the whole thing off with a black cowboy hat bedecked with a white jeweled band. As you can see in the photograph our little Frank Butler was magnificent, thanks to the generosity of his Mom.

Mix a little imagination with some good old-fashioned borrowing and you will be able to create many costumes at absolutely no cost. Millions of outfits lie in dusty attics of this fair land. Spread the word about what you need. For a particularly hard-to-find item, run an ad in your PTA newsletter. Long skirts always seem to be plentiful. We have been able to borrow a sport coat for the boy who needs but does not own one. Even if the loaned items are not perfect sizes for your children, often they can be tucked in here and there to make them fit. If the item is donated outright, take it apart and remake it for the child. In one of our shows, we had a pixie of a girl playing the part of a little boy. We borrowed a shirt for her from one of the boys in the cast. Someone donated a pair of outgrown pants so we cut them off below the knee, gathered in the leg at the cut-off point with elastic and made a perfect pair of knickers.

The one area where your imagination may fail you is shoes, the hardest item to find. Children these days live in sneakers, and many do not own dress shoes. Sneakers simply do not look appropriate for the time periods in many plays. Of course, Indians and urchins can always go barefooted unless your stage is splintery. Sometimes in desperation, we have borrowed dress shoes from children who had them for others who did not. Ballet slippers can be used and they are a handy addition to your costume closet.

Left: Annie Oakley is ready for high society in her sequined ball gown. Right: A reversible vest tops the costume of the dashing Frank Butler.

Ask parents to think of you when it is time to discard old ballet slippers or other items that could be used on stage. If your parents are aware of the types of outfits you are collecting, gradually your costume closet will grow into a gold mine of classic garments. Certain items, such as petticoats, long skirts and high-necked blouses will be used again and again. We have an admirable assortment of hats for both sexes. We also collect old jewelry, especially brooches which lend authenticity to period costumes when pinned to the neck of a blouse. A large necklace which can be looped around the top of a coathanger with the costume backstage and then popped over the head of the actress is satisfactory. Otherwise, use jewelry that can be permanently pinned to the costume. Avoid that which must be removed or added during the course of the play, particularly small pieces and earrings that are easily lost backstage.

Color Can Do Wonders

When planning costumes, think of color and how it interacts with the backdrop and other actors' clothing. Remember that costumes are little more than blocks of color as seen by the audience so let them do the work of creating the illusion you desire. Children who play parts of older characters should be dressed in darker colors, while those who play the parts of young people are dressed in bright colors.

Your male and female leads should be dressed in vivid colors so that they stand out from the other characters. Take care during the early planning stages that the colors chosen for your leads are coordinated and do not clash. The sight of the leading lady dressed in hot pink gazing into the eyes of the leading man dressed in burnt orange could be somewhat jarring. How much better it would be for her to be dressed in blue or pale green. Once we almost had two male secondary leads dressed in identical light blue. One parent thought of this in the nick of time and bought electric blue fabric instead, so we avoided the Blue Twins.

During one dress rehearsal when we saw the finished costumes all together for the first time, we found that most of the minor characters were dressed in white tops, girls in white blouses and boys in white shirts. They did not fade into the backdrop but they did look like they all shopped at the same dull clothing store. White can be drab when used in quantity. At that late date, we hurriedly rounded up bright scarves and sashes for the girls. To the boys' costumes we added colorful ties. That was the best we could do on short notice to remedy a problem we did not realize we had until it was almost too late. From then on we encouraged our casts to choose colored blouses and shirts, and now there is always a pleasing color mix.

A single hue worn by many dancers on stage makes a big impact so we try to choose a main color for the backdrop that will be harmonious with the dancers' costumes. In addition to the backdrop, be conscious of the shade of the side curtains on your stage. One year the junior high school, whose stage we were using, threw away their old neutral beige stage curtains and installed new ones which were a deep midnight blue, a big change! If our children had worn very dark costumes on that stage, they would have been invisible to the audience when viewed against those curtains. Luckily, we knew about this new addition long before the costumes were made, and we were able to advise parents to avoid dark colors.

The Quick Change

The last consideration in costume design is the ease and speed with which the attire can be changed. The tempo of your play must never be slowed by a long pause for clothing change. Consider too that backstage is often a dark, cramped space with little room for mass costume changing, let alone modesty. If a character is a minor one and he wears the same outfit throughout the play, this is not a problem. If, however, this character is your leading lady and she must be transformed from a dirty little waif into a high-fashion society lady in under one minute, then it becomes very important indeed.

Use every device you can think of to meet this challenge. Accessories can be a clever answer. The look of a simple costume can be totally changed by using many different accessories such as shawls, capes, vests, hats, sashes, ties, purses, scarves, aprons, collars, etc. Remember the reversible vest worn by our Frank Butler in *Annie Get Your Gun*. Such items are a boon to harried backstage help.

The heroine Maria in Rodgers and Hammerstein's *The Sound of Music* could begin the show at the abbey wearing her novice's uniform consisting of a simple gray dress with a white apron and black veil. For the next scene when she appears at the Von Trapp's front door, remove the apron and veil and add an old jacket to create her drab little outfit.

Sooner or later, though, Maria is going to have to change out of that gray dress, and it will be much easier and faster if it does not have 50 tiny buttons down the back. Even if your backstage crew has the dexterity of an octopus, buttons can be a nightmare. Ties are all right;

Annie Oakley's shabby outfit hides a stunning Wild West Show costume.

zippers are even better. The self-gripping fastening product sold by the yard in strips or in packages of small round discs is also a blessing to costume changing. If you *must* use buttons, make sure they are big.

Annie shows off her red Wild West Show costume to an impressed Frank Butler.

Take a tip from mountain climbers and use the layering technique. That way one outfit can be quickly removed to reveal another. It is much easier to snatch off costume No. 1 over the leading lady's head at the end of Scene 1 and immediately send her out for Scene 2 wearing costume No. 2 than to strip her down to her underwear between scenes. This works well as long as the first costume is looser, bulkier and slightly longer than the second. Our leading lady in *Annie Get Your Gun* started the show wearing a burlap gathered skirt and tan peasant bouse. Hidden under that was her next outfit, a white blouse and red velour skirt and matching vest, both trimmed with six-inch white fringe. When the time came to change, she had only to pull off the burlap skirt and peasant blouse, put on her cowboy boots and pop the red cowboy hat trimmed with white feathers on her head.

Think how much longer it would have taken her to put on the whole red outfit, too.

In a later scene, our Annie Oakley had to wear a fancy party dress. She ducked behind a three-cornered screen which we kept backstage for her costume changes and shed her red skirt and vest, hat and boots. To her white blouse she added a long white skirt, shoes and a scoop-necked sleeveless top covered with pearl sequins. The top was one of those treasures we uncovered in someone's attic and had trimmed to fit our Annie. A red taffeta sash loaded with her medals draped from shoulder to hip. This elegance was topped off by a rhinestone tiara loaned by another parent. Our Annie's costume glittered as much as her performance! (See page 87.)

In the same show, our cowboys and ladies were able to transform themselves into Indian dancers while confined to a small coed territory backstage, and maintain modesty at the same time. The Indian costumes consisted of loosely-fitting long-sleeved tops and full length pants. The boys simply slipped the suits over their cowboy outfits. The girls, who were all dressed in blouses and skirts, first put the Indian tops on over their blouses. Then they pulled the pants on under their long skirts and removed the skirts. An Indian headband for each dancer was packed with the costume. Changing was a fast operation, and the system worked well except for the first dress rehearsal. On that day the scene began too soon and the lead dancer appeared on stage with his Indian pants in his hand to a chorus of giggles from onlookers. After that the backstage crew always made sure everyone was completely in costume before the scene was allowed to begin.

Costume Committee

While the mechanics of costuming a play are not difficult, a Costume Committee is essential. The reason is that some parents do not sew, and they will need help making costumes for their children. These parents are generally hesitant even to purchase fabric for fear of choosing the wrong thing. The happy solution to this situation is that a seamstress on the Committee agrees to "adopt" a child whose parent does not sew. This adoption entails the purchasing, making and fitting of a costume for the child. The child's parent pays the seamstress directly for fabric and supplies. While no charge is made for the loving labor involved in sewing, one grateful father presented his child's seamstress with a bottle of fine wine.

The second important function of the Costume Committee is

cutting fabric from master patterns when many identical costumes are needed, as for a dance group. If your show requires such outfits, the saga of our Indian dance may help you organize the project. For *Annie Get Your Gun* we planned to feature 17 minor characters plus one solo dancer and a drummer in an Indian dance number. We wanted them all dressed in identical costumes. As dancers they needed suits which would allow them free movement and withstand the stresses dancing would place on the seams. They had to be loose enough to fit over and hide their other costumes which would be worn during the rest of the show. Jo Ann, our Costume Coordinator, found a pattern which seemed to fill the bill. It had a loosely-fitting top with long, raglan sleeves and a draw string neck. The pants were a loose pajama-like style with an elastic waistband. Both top and pants were trimmed with two-inch self-fringe. We would buy 19 Indian headbands with single feathers. After checking with the Scenery Chairman about colors to be used in the backdrop, Jo Ann chose a rust-colored velour fabric resembling buckskin.

The first step was to determine how many yards of the velour we would need. In measuring all the children we found that most were fairly close to two standard sizes. A few would need slightly longer sleeves or pant legs. We were careful to measure the sleeve length from shoulder to wrist on the outside, with the arm bent, so that the sleeve would not be too short. Jo Ann purchased the Indian patterns and traced them onto brown wrapping paper in two sizes using the originals as a guide. Then on a gridded cutting board marking off the expected fabric width, she experimented with placement of the two patterns. She found the arrangement which allowed the pieces to fit as closely together as possible and resulted in the least fabric waste. She then measured the length of the section of the cutting board covered by the two patterns to determine the yardage necessary for two costumes. That amount was multiplied by one-half the number of costumes needed. To that number she added two extra yards to allow a margin for error. Her calculations came to 56 yards and proved to be quite accurate.

We then entered into the period of fabric search mentioned earlier in this chapter when we discovered what a headache seasonal fabric can be. By the time the Costume Committee gathered for the "cutting bee" at the home of the Costume Coordinator, we were all acutely aware of what a precious commodity our velour was and we dared not waste a single scrap. Within two hours, ten mothers wielding shears had cut out 19 costumes and miles of fringe. Each set of costume pieces was packed with a copy of sewing instructions in a plastic bag and labeled with the dancer's name. Thread was not included. The next day those children whose parents could sew were given their costume bags. Those bags intended for children of non-sewing parents were held by the Costume Committee to be made by them. An extra bonus was the fun everyone had. During the course of that delightful evening, several parents who had arrived as strangers had the chance to become acquainted with the parents of their children's friends. The play thus paid another dividend to the community.

Specialty Accessories

Some plays will require specialty costume items for which a pattern will not be available. Such an item was the spats we wanted for the boys in one of our period plays. So a brave parent volunteered to make a pattern for us. Using scraps of fabric and the trial-and-error method, she finally succeeded. She sent the pattern to me, I duplicated it, and sent it home to the parents. They made spats and matching bow ties and our boys looked great!

One of the loveliest and most inventive accessories ever made was also the most hilarious. In *Annie Get Your Gun* Annie Oakley shoots a stuffed bird off of the hat of Dolly Tate. We decided the most sensible way to handle this trick was to allow Dolly to appear on stage wearing the hat with the bird perched on top. Then she would exit stage left, a shot would be heard, and Annie would enter stage right, looking around for the bird she had just shot. Dolly, outraged, marches on, still wearing the hat, but carrying the bird in her hand. There is no pause in the action. One thing happens right after the other. That bird had to be instantaneously removeable when Dolly came off stage so that she could come back on immediately with the bird in her hand.

Jo Ann, Costume Designer Extraordinaire, applied her genius to the challenge and came up with the perfect solution. She found a black straw hat with medium brim. At Christmas time, when such items were available, she purchased a large white dove. She sewed a circle of ½-inch wide elastic to the crown of the hat and slipped the dove into it. To hide the elastic, decorate the hat and also keep the hat on the child's head, she used white nylon netting. It made a pretty "nest" for the bird, hiding the elastic at the crown, and was pulled over the brim and tied under Dolly's chin in a big bow. Dolly wore the hat in the first part of the scene, bird in elastic. When she exited and the shot was heard, the bird was quickly slipped out of the elastic and Dolly rushed back on stage carrying it. The audience loved it!

Beautiful Dolly Tate in her white dove hat — is outraged when Annie Oakley mistakenly shoots the dove right off.

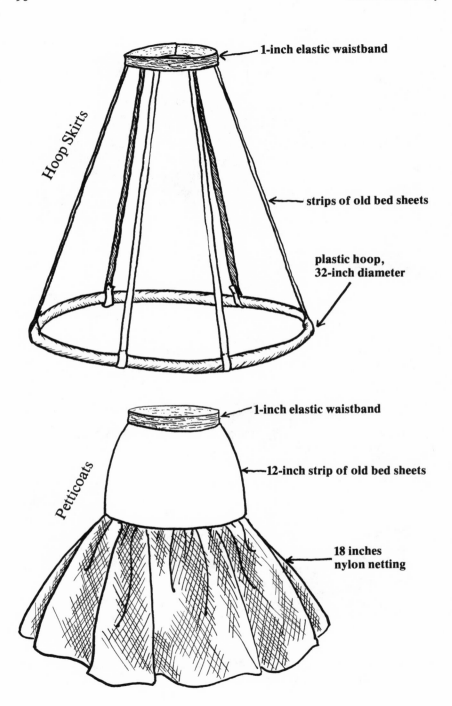

1-inch elastic waistband

Hoop Skirts

strips of old bed sheets

**plastic hoop,
32-inch diameter**

1-inch elastic waistband

Petticoats

12-inch strip of old bed sheets

**18 inches
nylon netting**

Hoop Skirts and Petticoats

Another play was set in an era one hundred years ago. Our ladies needed hoop skirts. The hoop skirts rage of the fifties had come and gone and we could not locate a single hoop. Fortunately, the physical education teacher in our school had among her athletic equipment a number of large plastic hoops. The children would twirl them around their bodies, keeping them in motion with their swivel hip gyrations. She was not using the hoops in her classes at the time so she loaned them to us for two months. A very creative gal on our Costume Committee turned them into hoop skirts. She tore long strips of fabric from old bedsheets and attached six strips evenly around an elastic waistband. The other end of the strips was looped around the hoops and sewn in place at ankle length. Presto! Hoop skirts!

One valuable addition to our costume closet was petticoats made from nylon netting. They are used year after year. Using funds donated by the PTA, we purchased 24 yards of white nylon netting, 36 inches in width. Ten year old girls are not very tall and by using a dropped-hip style each petticoat required a small amount of netting. The netting was cut in half lengthwise. One inch elastic served as the waistband to which was attached a 12-inch band of old bedsheet muslin. The netting was gathered and stitched to the bottom of the sheeting. Had the netting been attached directly to the elastic waistband, not only would we have been able to make fewer petticoats, but they would have felt extremely scratchy to the girls as well.

Makeup

Stage makeup is a must. Even the newscasters on television must wear it. Without it, under the stage lights, they would appear washed out — almost dead. Children also look pale on stage so plan on using makeup. During the early months of planning for the show, I always notify my boys that they must wear it, just as the girls do. It takes them some time to get used to the idea. Eventually, they decide that if it's good enough for their heroes on television, it's good enough for them.

Even though our makeup is kept fairly simple, the children are too young to apply it to themselves. At the Parents' Meeting recruit volunteers for the Makeup Committee who will apply the cosmetics in an assembly line fashion before the dress rehearsal and before all performances. One parent should head the committee and handle scheduling. You will probably need six to eight parents to handle the job for

35 to 45 children at each performance. Older teenage sisters love to help out for the evening performance.

Cosmetics are expensive. If yours is a no-budget production, send the parents a list of your specific makeup needs and ask them to send in makeup they have but do not want. You'll be pleasantly surprised at the donations you'll receive. When you graduate to a small budget, you can purchase whatever you need. Watch newspaper ads for cosmetic sales. Take advantage of less expensive brands carried by most drug stores.

The makeup we usually use is (1) face powder, (2) rouge, (3) lipstick, (4) eye shadow and (5) eye liner.

Two or three compacts of pressed powder in a rosy tint will be adequate for a half dozen performances. If the powder is donated, buy new inexpensive powder puffs.

Use the powder-type rouge instead of cream. It goes on easily and quickly with less unevenness of color. Have one light pink powder rouge for the boys and a darker shade for the girls. Applying it with a three-inch powder puff is easier and quicker than using the regular applicator.

Use two shades of lipstick, a light pink for the boys and a darker shade for the girls. Avoid bright red or plum because they are too overpowering on children. Provide at least two tubes of lipstick for the boys and two for the girls and make sure they are labeled. You will not use a whole tube of lipstick per show, but the Stage Manager always keeps one of each shade in her apron pocket during performances. Some children lick off their lipstick during a show and the Stage Manager makes repairs. Dotting rather than smearing the lipstick on works best for children. If the thought of one tube of lipstick being applied to 30 mouths makes some germ-conscious mother squeamish or if a child has a known infection, that child may purchase a lipstick for his own use.

Eye shadow for boys is beige or brown. For girls use blue or green to coordinate with their costumes. Apply eye liner to the upper lid only. Children's eyes tend to water when liner is applied to the lower lids. Use eye brow pencil on children with light or scanty brows.

Except for red-headed children, we do not use mascara. It takes too much time to apply and the children frequently smudge it before it is dry. Also, many children are allergic to mascara, and red, swollen, itching eyes you can do without! Red heads do need mascara since their eyelashes are so light that they are invisible to the audience.

Once in a while we use dark pancake makeup. The beautiful girl who played Chief Sitting Bull in our *Annie Get Your Gun* needed a darker skin tone. We purchased pancake makeup in an "Egyptian"

Dark pancake makeup and a huge feathered headdress turn a beautiful girl into Chief Sitting Bull.

shade. We applied it with a wet sponge, covering her face, ears, neck and hands. She wore a long sleeved shirt, so her arms were not exposed. As soon as the makeup dried, she dressed in her costume with huge feathered headdress and was transformed into a very believable Indian Chief.

Perhaps the trickiest problem we ever had was how to make our Anglo-Saxon children look Oriental. None of the products we tried achieved the almond-eyed look we hoped for. Finally we settled for changing the shape of the eyebrows. Instead of eyebrows that dropped down at the outer edges, we wanted ours to go up slightly. We covered the children's eyebrows from the center point to the outer edges with a product intended to cover facial blemishes. Then we drew on new eyebrows with black grease pencils purchased from a theatrical supply store, which we located through the Yellow Pages of the phone book. The result: Oriental-looking children.

Keep trying different applications until you achieve the look you desire. Always try your makeup out on four or more children with the stage lights shining on them *before* dress rehearsal. Makeup that looks fine in the daylight may be too pale under the stage lights. You may discover that the lipstick or rouge shade you had thought perfect is all wrong. You may have to adjust powder shades for Oriental or black children. Have all of these details worked out before you instruct your parent volunteers who will make up the entire cast. Be sure to use makeup at one dress rehearsal so that things will run smoothly at the student performance. Follow the procedure below.

Makeup Stations

When the day of your first performance dawns, you should arrive and set up the makeup area at least 1½ hours before the performance time. Makeup is applied by an assembly line system. Lay out supplies on a large table, forming six stations, three on each side of the table. Children will line up at one corner of the table and proceed around it from one makeup station to the next. In the center of the table place a big box of facial tissues and several large bath towels to be wrapped around the children's shoulders to keep the powder off their costumes. A large paper bag goes under the table for trash.

Station No. 1 will be powder. As soon as the adult at that station has patted the powder onto their faces, the children proceed to station No. 2, which is rouge. Station No. 3 is lipstick, No. 4 is eye shadow and No. 5 is eyeliner. Stations No. 3 and 5 should have two adults experienced with makeup assigned to them because lipstick and eyeliner take longer to apply.

Station No. 6 is for hair. Supply that station with two hairbrushes, a comb, bobby pins, hair pins, rubber bands and hair spray. This station is for ordinary hair brushing needs. Assign someone away from the table to handle special hair jobs. Girls with long hair who play boys' parts will need extra help putting up their hair. Using this system, you should be able to put makeup on 35 faces in 45 minutes. Even 45 faces take only an hour. If you have more children, adjust your time schedule accordingly or set up a second table with the same stations.

Approximately 1¼ hours before the performance, parent makeup volunteers should arrive and be given their instructions. The soloists and the girls in the cast also arrive for costuming. As soon as they have finished dressing, they immediately report to the makeup table. Soloists are permitted to go to the head of the line so that they can finish quickly and then report to the Musical Director who will warm up their voices. One hour before performance, the boys in the cast arrive, dress and report for makeup. Fifteen minutes before performance time, the entire cast reports to the Director for a last minute pep talk. Five minutes before the performance the cast walks to the stage. Right on time the show begins! Excitement! Applause! Pride!

X

Scenery

Good scenery can add a special flair to your show. It can fill the stage with color to create a mood. It can make the fantasy created by the actors more believable. The right kind of adult planning and preparation can enable your children to produce beautiful and professional-looking scenery. The results will be amazing, and your youngsters will proudly boast to their friends that, "I painted that!"

While you are choosing the script and modifying it for your youngsters during the summer months, consider the scenery needs along with all of the other aspects of the play. In fact, scenery requirements may determine whether or not you will be able to produce a particular play. A show requiring many elaborate and drastically different sets may be impossible to manage due to physical or economic limitations. If you really have your heart set on such a show though, consider whether all of the different sets are vital to the story line. Sometimes certain ones can be dropped or action moved to a central area, without affecting the plot. Remember that changing scenery takes time. Too many changes slow the pace and break the flow of the show. A little judicious simplification may solve the problem. Try to limit sets to two or three main ones at most. If you are blessed with a curtained stage, short scenes can be done in front of the curtain. Train or boat scenes are examples.

If you come upon a technical snag, talk it over with your scenery chairman if you already have one. Two heads are always better than one in working out thorny challenges. Consider these things:

- ► Does most of the action happen indoors or out of doors? Can it be simplified to occur mainly in one or the other?
- ► Do you need any buildings separate from the backdrop, such as a house or barn? Or could the buildings be painted into the backdrop?

▶ Does some of the action occur on a vehicle such as a train, stagecoach or boat?

In one of our shows, most of the action took place in a town square setting. However, two scenes were supposed to happen in the local high school gymnasium. After wrestling with the question of how to create a gymnasium, I suddenly realized that the location of those two scenes had absolutely nothing to do with the story. We played the scenes in the town square, and they worked perfectly!

Scenery for Kids

After your parents' meeting in October and the return of the parent signup forms, you should have a Scenery Designer and committee. You and the Designer must begin to work out precisely what will be created and how. As with each phase of this project, the scenery must be designed and made with children in mind. Generally, it must be:

▶ Lightweight and durable enough to be handled by stage crew children.

▶ Economical to make.

▶ Repairable, since accidents do happen.

▶ Compatible with your stage facilities.

▶ Easy to put up and take down.

▶ Easily transported, if you plan to take your show to other locations.

Check the library for books about Broadway plays. Many have photographs of scenery for specific shows and may be a rich source of ideas. Theater craft books are helpful. They are filled with ideas for marvelous sets including everything from a few cleverly handled lights to huge motorized sets elaborately depicting riverboats, trains or mountains. Obviously, such sophisticated sets are not for your children but they can provide ideas which you may be able to adapt to meet your needs.

For your purposes, the simplest, most effective and flexible technique is the use of a single paper backdrop and a reversible flat. A backdrop is a huge sheet of paper, painted with your central scene and attached to the rear wall or curtain of the stage. A flat is a free-standing frame, usually measuring 4 × 6 feet, to which is attached paper, painted to depict whatever structure you require. For one of our shows our backdrop was a rural outdoor scene, and the reversible flat had a little house painted on one side and a barn on the other. We thereby created three stage sets.

By December you and the Scenery Designer will have a clear idea of what each scene will require in the way of scenery and will have worked out the specifics. If scenery is not your area of expertise and if you have complete faith in your Scenery Designer, let her take over. Make sure she is fully aware of the time schedule for your show. You will wish to schedule Scenery Painting Day during February if possible so that things do not become too rushed later when rehearsals are drawing to a busy conclusion. Of course, you will keep in touch with all of your chairmen, Scenery Designer included, in case they need help of any kind.

Backdrop

A paper backdrop can be made in such a way that it fulfills all the requirements of student scenery. It can be made from readily available, economical materials. It is lightweight and can be hung at the rear of your stage, unchanged throughout the performance. It is easily painted by children. It may show either an indoor scene, such as a palace throne room, or an outdoor scene, such as a mountainside. It can be rolled up and transported in a station wagon or van. It can be mended with paper or cloth tape. Perfect!

Once you have decided on approximately what your backdrop will look like, the next step is to measure the area to be covered by it. If you have a curtained stage, the paper backdrop can be pinned easily to the rear curtain, using macrame T-pins. Be sure to measure the width of the *rear* of the stage, since some stages are trapezoid in shape, narrower at the rear than at the front. If you measure the stage front and cut your backdrop accordingly, when the time comes to hang it, you may make the unhappy discovery that it is too wide. The year this happened to me, the backdrop was about 2 feet too wide on each side, so it wrapped around the corners, closing off the rear curtain openings and making it impossible for our young actors to use these areas for entrances and exits.

If you perform only on a portable, folding stage in the school gymnasium or cafeteria, the backdrop should match its width. If you will be using two different stages, the size should match the larger stage. First, decide on the placement of the stage. Take into consideration the space you may need for seating the audience and cast, storage of props needed during the show, room for changing costumes and such. You may wish to create "wings" to hide those activities by using screens on either side of the stage. Conveniently located closets or hallways nearby may also serve as dressing rooms.

Once the decision of stage placement is made, examine the wall behind it. If it is made of cork or some other bulletin board material, it will be easy to tack or staple the backdrop to the wall. If the wall is cinderblock, tape or staples will probably not work. The best system in that case is to nail a line of 1 × 3 inch × 6 foot furring strips to the wall. The backdrop paper can be tacked or stapled to that wooden strip.

Attach the strip to the wall with masonry nails at a height of 9 feet above the level of the stage floor, or whatever height you expect your backdrop to be. If you are not up to this task, prevail upon the good nature of one of the children's dads to give you a hand. It might also be prudent for you to clear this job with the school principal beforehand.

Using a Grid

Once you have determined the content and size of the backdrop, the next step is to draw a small sketch of how it will actually look. Try to do this job in December or January, if not before. It should be drawn to scale, allowing 1 inch to 1 foot of the finished backdrop. An easy way to do this is by the use of a grid. Then the design can be transferred easily, block by block, to the backdrop paper. If you have never tried this method, you will be pleased to discover what a labor-saving device a grid is.

On medium white paper, using a medium width pen, draw a grid with 1 inch squares scaled in the same dimensions as the finished backdrop. For example, if your backdrop is to be 9 feet high and 21 feet long, draw a rectangle 9 inches high and 21 inches wide, with each 1 inch space indicated by a vertical or horizontal line. Number each line from left to right and top to bottom in sequence. It will resemble an odd checkerboard.

Over the grid, sketch the backdrop design. The inked grid will endure many erasures and will simplify the job of sketching by providing handy horizontals and verticals, reducing the chore of measuring.

As you are designing, keep in mind that the scenery should be scaled to the height of the children in the cast. Buildings, doorways,

Stage arrangement.

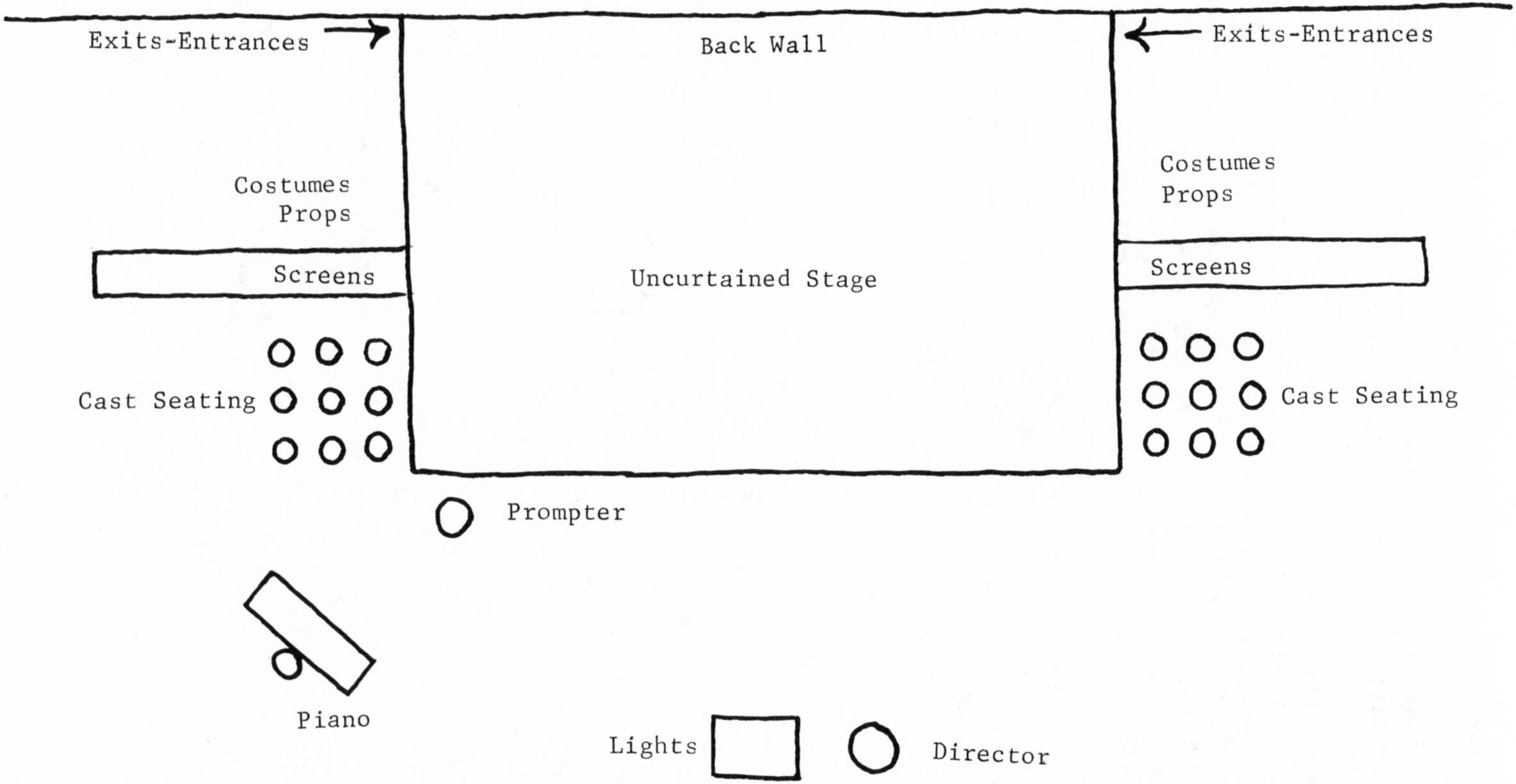

Exits–Entrances

Back Wall

Exits–Entrances

Costumes
Props

Screens

Cast Seating

○ ○ ○
○ ○ ○
○ ○ ○

Uncurtained Stage

Prompter
○

Costumes
Props

Screens

○ ○ ○
○ ○ ○
○ ○ ○

Cast Seating

Piano

Lights

Director
○

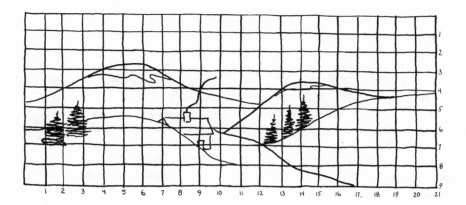

Grid and scenery sketch.

fences, etc. should appear to be appropriately sized as if the actors were adults.

If the average height of your cast is 4 feet, then ordinary door-ways should be at least that height. If your stage is very deep and the eye level of the audience is low, doorways and other structures may appear lower than they actually are. Also, the short curtains, called teasers, hanging from the ceiling of a curtained stage may hide the top few inches of the backdrop.

If the backdrop calls for a landscape or architectural detail with which you are unfamiliar, check with your friend, the librarian, for a book on the subject. The children, caught up in the play and its back-ground, will be doing research on geography, culture or history of the location or the time period.

You do want to try to be as accurate as you possibly can be with your scenery.

In addition, the library is full of simple how-to art books. A quick study of perspective may be helpful if you have never before thought about horizons or vanishing points. This is the old railroad track-into-the-sunset principle, which demonstrates that parallel lines converge as they go away from the eye. Another hint: An outdoor scene will be more artistically pleasing and look less like a sandwich if you do not put the horizon line, the line where the sky meets the earth, in the precise center between the top and the bottom of the backdrop. As helpful as the art books may be, don't be frightened by the rules. If talk of perspective intimidates you, just stay away from complicated angles and plan a simple backdrop which avoids all those problems. If you like the way something looks, even if it does not do exactly what the book says it should, use it anyway.

The best piece of advice I can give you about your scenery design is KEEP IT SIMPLE. Avoid a lot of fussy details. They will not be visible to the audience anyway and will complicate the job of painting. You will want to create an impression and to enhance the acting and costumes by providing an attractive and complementary background.

You do not want the backdrop to be so distracting that it jars the audience's attention away from the most important thing on the stage—the children. Nevertheless, have fun with this job. Let your imagination soar! Here is the chance to create something huge and beautiful. Just think how many artists would love to have 189 square feet of their work on public display!

Paper for the backdrop should be of medium-heavy weight, so that it will be durable and will withstand frequent handling. Paint should not be able to soak through it, and it should not buckle too much when painted. Obviously white is the best color choice. Many schools stock large rolls of heavy paper approximately 36 inches in width.

You can use such paper by taping sheets of it together with miles of 2 inch masking tape. It is a tedious job but if your budget is non-existent and the paper is free, it can be done satisfactorily. Be sure to tape it *before* you paint, while the paper is still flat and the edges are even. The paint, when applied, should not loosen the tape.

If you are lucky enough to have a small budget, the best paper to buy for the backdrop is background paper sold at photographic supply stores. It is used by professional photographers as background material. It is available in 9 foot widths by 36 foot lengths, in white and other colors. It has a nice weight but tends to be slightly soft and easily torn at the edges. Therefore, your first task as soon as the paper is out of the box and cut to size is to reinforce the edges by applying 2 inch masking tape all the way around on the back. In fact, two rows of tape at the bottom and top and three rows on either side are even better. The tape helps the paper resist curling after painting and makes the edges strong enough to withstand youngsters tripping over them as they paint.

Once the design is finished, transfer it to the backdrop paper by following the grid, block by block. If your work area is smaller than the total length of the backdrop, you will have to work in sections,

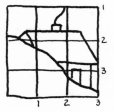

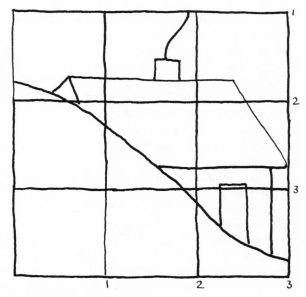

Transferring the design.

rolling and unrolling the paper from one side to the other. The first step is to grid the backdrop paper with a pencil in the same manner as your 1 inch grid, using 1 foot blocks instead. Number the horizontals and verticals as you did the smaller grid. Complicated designs require a complete grid. Later as you become more experienced, some backdrops, including vast areas of sky for example, probably will not require a complete grid. In the beginning, it is best to play it safe and draw the entire grid. A reasonably straight 6 foot furring strip makes a great drawing aid for this job. Measure off 1 foot segments at the top and bottom of the paper and then line up the furring strip between the pairs of marks and draw a line along its edge.

Next you will draw the background design onto the backdrop paper. The grid will make it easy. Using a pencil, draw the design one block at a time, matching the larger version to the smaller. For example, if a line of the smaller version in block Number 1 goes from the lower left corner of the square to the upper right corner, simply draw it that way on the larger version.

T-squares, angles and other drawing devices are handy if you have them. If you don't, your house is full of other items which work well, such as yardsticks or books. Art supply stores sell a compass which is slipped over a yardstick for drawing circles up to 2 yards in diameter.

The same thing can be accomplished by tying a string to a pencil and holding the free end of the string to the paper with the thumb while swinging the pencil in an arc. Smaller circles can be drawn easily using household items such as tape rolls, dishes, even lamp shades, as patterns. Special shapes, such as the points of a wrought iron fence or gingerbread trim of a house, can be repeated identically by making a cardboard pattern and tracing around it.

If you make a mistake, either erase or scribble it out. If you do erase, try to brush the eraser dust away since any grit under the paper can puncture it as you kneel on it to draw. Incidentally, if you use garden knee pads, you can ease the stress of kneeling on the hard floor for a long time.

This part of the job is the most fun. It is very exciting to see your design actually begin to take shape. Once the design is completely drawn, use a black felt-tipped marker to highlight the lines of the man-made structures. Use an appropriately colored marker for trees, mountains, etc. since paint seldom covers the black marker completely, and you wouldn't want a black line around objects of nature. When finished, the backdrop will resemble a large page in a child's coloring book.

Choosing Color and Paint

You have probably been thinking all along about the colors you might want to use, but now is the time to make the final decisions. You must consider not only the impression made by the color of the backdrop, but also the color's interaction with the costumes and props on stage.

The Scenery Designer and Costume Coordinator may wish to devise a harmonious color scheme. Bright red Indian costumes against an orange circus tent would never do! The colors must work together, drawing the eye into the scene and leading it naturally to the action of the play.

We live with color all our lives, but how many people really think about the effect it has on them? Warm colors, such as red and orange, send a message of happiness, excitement and action. Visually they advance toward the audience's eye. Cooler colors, such as blue and green, seem to recede from the audience and have a lazy, calming effect. Use this knowledge to create the right mood for your particular show.

Choose your paint with your young painters and your budget in mind. Schools usually stock non-toxic water based tempera paint, powder or premixed, in basic colors, but for scenery painting it has certain disadvantages. Its most annoying aspect is the nasty habit of flaking off the paper once it has dried, particularly if the paint is applied thickly and the paper is rolled after painting. Your backdrop will almost certainly have to be rolled up since few schools or homes have room enough to leave a 9 foot × 21 foot backdrop lying about. The flaking problem can be overcome to a certain extent by adding a bit of ordinary white latex wall paint to the tempera, which seems to give the finished paint a more flexible quality. Buy a gallon of the cheapest kind of latex you can find. By adding it to the tempera or even using the latex as a base and adding the tempera as a tint, the finished painted surface will have enough flexibility that you will be able to curl the backdrop into a roll having a 12 inch diameter without worrying about flaking. The addition of latex to the paint will mean that spills may not wash out of clothing as readily as plain tempera paint, so be sure to warn the children to wear old clothes on Scenery Painting Day.

The second annoying feature of tempera paint is that results are sometimes unpredictable when mixing two primary colors. The primary colors are red, yellow and blue as shown on the Color Wheel (see illustration). Theoretically, you should be able to mix any other color from those three. However, mixing clear blue tempera with clear yellow tempera does not necessarily result in the expected lovely green. This quirk seems to be related to the chemistry involved in the manufacture of the paint. You will just have to experiment with different combinations of colors to find the one you want. Keep track of the proportions, rather like a recipe, and after making up several samples, choose the one that seems best for your purposes.

After you have mixed up a few paint samples, try them out on a small rough sketch of your scenery to be sure the colors work well together. Generally, it is best to avoid pure undiluted paint colors in the backdrop. They are too intense and will fight your costumed actors for attention. Tone them down either by adding white for a more pastel shade and/or add a touch of the color opposite it on the Color Wheel to achieve a grayed tone. Then touches of pure color can be used in the costumes for a harmonious and pleasing effect. Stage lights can do tricky things to colors too.

Related colors near each other on the Color Wheel, such as purple and blue, can be used together in large quantities. Sometimes a monochromatic color scheme, using shades of a single color such as yellow, gold and brown, can be done in a very striking fashion.

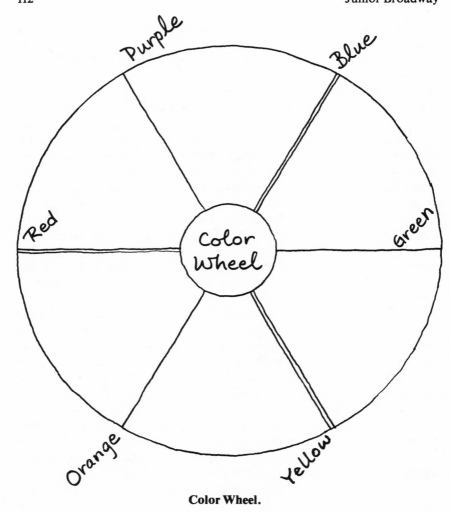

Color Wheel.

Contrasting colors are those opposite each other on the Color Wheel, such as red and green. Using large and nearly equal areas of contrasting colors is seldom pleasing to the eye. Save the contrasts for highlights and for costumes.

Once you have decided on all of the colors, number each one on a chart. Our backdrops have had from twelve to thirty different shades, and the children have handled them well. Now go back to the backdrop and number each area, indicating the color to be used. You are creating a gigantic paint-by-number picture. Use a red pencil for the paint numbers, so that the children will not be confused by other numbers and markings you may have used during measuring and sketching. Red pencil marks stand out but are easily covered, even by light paint colors.

Scenery Painting Day

It is almost time for your young painters to get into the act. Schedule Scenery Painting Day in February, and remind the children to wear old clothes. Friday is a good choice since the paint can dry thoroughly over the weekend before the paper is rolled up. Mix the paint a day or two ahead. If you do this too far in advance, the paint may become moldy or the can may rust and stain the paint.

Each paint color will be mixed according to the color chart and placed in an empty 1 pound coffee can. The best source for cans is a parent who works in an office with a small coffee maker. One pound coffee cans are ideal for this purpose. They are a size that is easy for youngsters to handle, and those nice tight plastic lids keep the paint from drying out. Attach a piece of masking tape to the side of the can and, with a felt-tipped marker, indicate the paint number on the tape and also on the plastic lid. Since you want to have as many children as possible painting simultaneously, you will need more than one can of some colors, particularly those which cover large areas. Those colors can be mixed in a large plastic household bucket and then poured into several coffee cans and labeled. Be sure to have on hand some empty cans as well. Some painting situations are easier if two painters working on one area can each have a can of paint. Just pour a little of the original supply into a spare can. However, be sure to label that can right away. Some shades are so similar that they are difficult to identify later.

Scenery Painting Day will be easier if you remember to bring along a few basic survival supplies. Besides paper, paint and brushes, you will need long handled spoons, such as iced teaspoons, to stir up the paint just before it is used. It settles quickly, even overnight. A roll of paper towels or a good supply of rags may be worth their weight in gold if one of your Rembrandts is butter-fingered! Pencils, masking tape, felt markers and big plastic garbage bags for trash also come in handy. Tall cans, such as 46 ounce juice cans, are nice for soaking dirty brushes, but don't leave the brushes standing on their bristles too long or they may be ruined. Ordinary ½ inch school art brushes are adequate for this job, although a few old 2 inch latex brushes will speed the job of a large area in a single color. I usually ask children to bring these in if they have them.

Bring along newspapers, too, but they will probably be necessary only around the edges of the backdrop, not under the entire piece. To be on the safe side, check to be certain the paint will not seep through the paper. Of course, several thicknesses of newspaper will be put under cans of paint during mixing.

When the great moment arrives, roll out the backdrop and enjoy the ooh's and aah's of the children as they marvel at your wonderful drawing! You will need a room large enough to spread the entire backdrop flat on the floor, with room around the edges for easy walking back and forth. We use a classroom and move the desks out into the hall temporarily.

Your young painters will be very excited and anxious to plunge into the project. Hold them back for a few more moments. Show them the sketches and color charts, so that they will know what the finished product should look like. Then announce a few simple tips for a successful venture. Better yet, furnish the Teacher-Director with a list of these tips ahead of time, so she can discuss them with the children when they are less excited and thus better able to absorb directions. Then on Scenery Painting Day, your announcement will add emphasis to each tip.

- ► Everyone must remove his shoes so that the paper will not be torn.
- ► Begin painting in the middle of the backdrop and work toward the outside edges.
- ► Watch out for your neighbor, his brush and his can of paint!
- ► Make sure the number on your can of paint matches the red number marked on the scenery.
- ► Stay inside the black marker lines. This is just like kindergarten when you first were told to, "Color inside the lines."
- ► Apply the paint in an even, thin coat, making sure it completely covers the paper but avoiding globs of paint.
- ► Brush in every direction and avoid scrubbing the paper with the brush since you might wear a hole in it.
- ► Rinse your brush *thoroughly* in water before you begin painting with a new color. The old color could muddy up the new one.
- ► When you are not sure about something, don't guess. Ask!

Opposite: Working head-to-head, many children can paint the backdrop simultaneously with outstanding results.

Assign each child an area near the center of the backdrop, and the group may begin painting. By having two rows of painters kneel head-to-head in the center with their feet toward the outside edges, as many as 25 children may paint a 9 × 21 foot backdrop simultaneously without problems, and they will probably finish in under two hours. Especially skilled child-artists may be assigned intricate areas.

The paper may pucker a bit when it is wet, but most of the puckers will disappear as the paint dries. Those that remain will never be noticed by the audience. Have several parents or other helpers on hand to answer questions, wash brushes and distribute paint cans. Discipline will not be a problem, since the children will be totally and happily absorbed in the job of painting.

I have done four backdrops with this technique and have never had a can of paint knocked over or a major rip in the paper. All of the children have been thrilled to have had a part in the project, and they proudly show their share of the finished masterpiece to their friends. "That's my fence!" "Those are my flowers!" They adopt the backdrop as their very own creation and become very protective of it, even standing guard over it to prevent other children in school from coming too close.

Make sure the paint is completely dry before you try to roll up the backdrop. During the painting some paint will have slopped over onto the marker lines. The black lines seem to bring out the details of buildings, fences and other man-made structures, so you may wish to sharpen up those lines. Trees, flowers, mountains and other natural features will not be outlined. If you are an especially brave and artistic Scenery Designer, you may even be willing to highlight, shade or texture the backdrop to give it a more three dimensional, realistic look. This should be done with a very light touch, however, since the children will be offended if they think someone has changed their creation.

Whether you have decided to secure the backdrop to the wall or back curtain of your stage with pins, tacks or staples, they can be driven through the upper edge of the paper, since it is well reinforced with masking tape. However, if you plan to take your show to several locations and the backdrop is to be put up several times, eventually the pins will wear holes in the paper which may become noticeable to the audience. A little trick to avoid that problem is to devise tabs attached to the top of the backdrop which can be pinned or tacked, leaving the masterpiece itself untouched. Use 2 inch wide cloth-backed duct tape. Cut a piece approximately 12 inches long. Stick the lower 6 inches to the back of the top edge of the backdrop. Then fold over the remaining

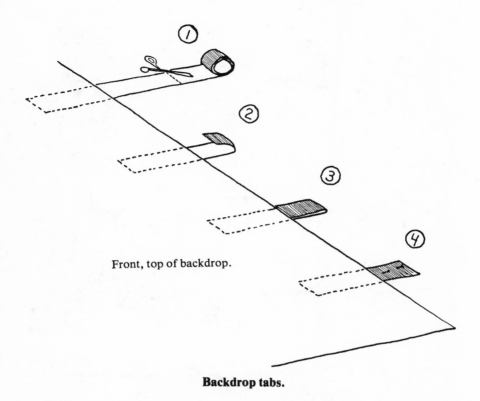

Front, top of backdrop.

Backdrop tabs.

6 inches on itself, forming a 3 inch tab. Space the tabs across the top edge every 18 inches or so. We always use these tabs on our backdrops to avoid any damage to our wonderful work of art.

Now the backdrop is ready whenever you need it. Roll it loosely and tie it with string for storage. If it must be carried outside on a rainy day, protect it from water spots by wrapping it in a painter's plastic drop cloth, 9 × 12 feet. You will probably hang the backdrop the week of your first dress rehearsal. This job will best be handled by adults, since it will involve the use of tall ladders to reach the top of the backdrop.

The Flat

The chances are that you will need more than just a single backdrop for your entire show. Lightweight flats give you versatility and are

Opposite, top: free-standing topiary trees add interest to the Wilson House, which was painted on the backdrop; bottom: by using two fences and a different entranceway on the flat, the Wilson House becomes the Wild West Show tent.

This page: reversible fences and flat transform the Wilson House into the Hotel Brevoort.

easily made. A flat is a light, free-standing wooden frame to which is stapled the same kind of paper used for the backdrop, painted in the desired design. Ours measures 4 feet wide × 6 feet high. If you purchase backdrop paper, there should be plenty left over for the flat after you have cut your backdrop. The flat can be one-sided or reversible. It can be made to look like almost anything, a small house for instance, or it can be used against the backdrop to change its appearance. Our *Annie Get Your Gun* had scenes requiring three distinctly different large buildings: a summer hotel, a city hotel and a large fairgrounds tent. We created all three with only one backdrop and one reversible flat.

First, the children painted a large summer hotel across the backdrop. The detail of the entranceway and door was concentrated in a 4 × 6 foot central area. The building itself was a nondescript shape. The roof had four peaks from which flags flew. We used the reversible flat, also painted by the children, to change the appearance of the summer hotel and thus produce the other two structures by positioning the flat directly in front of the doorway of the backdrop. One side of the flat had the New York hotel entrance, and the other showed a tent flap entrance for the fairgrounds tent. By using topiary trees, fences and other props, we made three distinctly different sets, using very little actual scenery.

If you decide to build a flat, start out by giving some thought to size. This is determined by the physical limitations of your performing area and by the vehicle in which you must transport it. If your stage is small, the flat must not be so big that it leaves no room for dancing and other stage action. If you expect to be invited to perform at some place other than your base location, be certain the flat will fit into the station wagons or vans of the parents who will be moving scenery. The children must be able to move it easily through a doorway. A flat, 4 feet wide × 6 feet high is a good size and can be constructed so that it balances well and is light enough for the stage crew to handle easily.

Who will construct the flat? While you may not be blessed with a professional cabinetmaker within your parent pool, you are bound to have at least one weekend carpenter who will take pity on you and lend a hand.

Building the flat does not require fine workmanship. After all, it will be invisible behind the painted paper cover. However, it must be sturdy, stand straight and balance itself.

A simple rectangular frame built with 1 × 3 inch × 6 foot furring strips will do nicely. A strip across the middle will strengthen the frame and make it less likely to warp. The strips are wide enough to

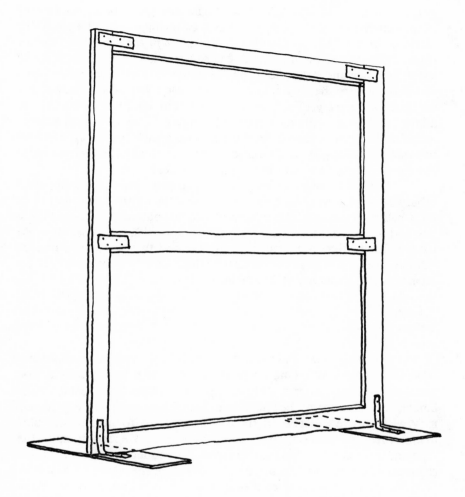

Flat, 4 × 6 feet, showing nailer plates and 6 × 21 inch footings, with metal angle.

allow the paper to be stapled on easily. One of your parents may have some scrap lumber left over from a household project and be willing to donate it to a worthy cause. One way to reinforce the corners is by using an item available at most hardware stores called a splice plate or nailer plate. It is a flat piece of metal with small holes, which is laid over the two pieces of wood to be joined, and nails are driven through the holes. Your carpenter may have other good ideas.

The question of feet to hold the flat upright is best answered by examining the particular use to be made of the flat. Will it be one-sided or reversible? Will it stand close to a wall? Will there be dancing performed on the stage while the flat is on, and is the dancing likely to cause the stage and flat to bounce? Since we use our flat year after year, we wanted it to be as versatile as possible. We never know what requirements next year's show will have, and we want to be able to adapt our flat accordingly. The easiest system is to make two 6 × 21 inch feet from plywood or rigid metal, and attach them to the flat by screwing metal angles to the flat and the feet. Paint the feet the same color as your stage so that they won't be noticeable.

If the flat has a tendency to bounce during a dance number or otherwise seems unstable, make a sandbag to place on each foot, out of sight behind the flat. Children's sandbox sand placed in a heavy plastic bag and sealed with a home sealing machine works well. The bags sold with such machines are especially durable and two such bags, one inside the other, are almost indestructible unless they snag on an especially sharp metal bolt or other object.

Ships

Your show may call for a shipboard scene, and there are several ways to suggest a ship. One way is to lay the 4 × 6 foot flat on its side and paint on the paper a ship's railing, complete with cleats, ropes, barrels, etc. Of course, the flat will not look like a complete ship so you may wish to use a darkened stage and spotlight for this scene, particularly if it involves only one or two characters. Depending upon the type and vintage of the ship in the scene, props such as fishing nets, sea chests, anchors and sails could be used to soften the edges of the flat by arranging the props in order of decreasing height and fading into the darkness at the edges of the spotlighted area.

If you have a curtained stage, you can play the scene in front of the curtain and suggest the ship using props alone. Wharves can be constructed from cardboard and held erect by attaching them to dowels anchored in large cans filled with concrete.

The Feet in Concrete Trick

We borrowed this concrete trick from gangster novels, and it is a super way to support any small piece of scenery such as a bush,

A "ship" using flat and props.

tombstone, sign or topiary tree. Note one of the snapshots of our set for *Annie Get Your Gun* on page 118.

The topiary trees we used are constructed (see page 124) using this method. Paint whatever you need on cardboard and attach it to a dowel or piece of scrap wood. Pound three or four nails into the base of the dowel and anchor it in ready-mix concrete placed in 3 pound cans, such as shortening cans. The nails help to hold the dowel in the concrete. The ready-mix concrete is available at the hardware store, mixes with a garden hoe and hardens quickly. A 67 pound sack will fill about 10 cans. The concrete is heavy enough that the can will definitely not tip over on stage. Paint the cans and dowels with bits of leftover paint you have tucked away in your basement. The cans can be made nearly invisible by painting them to match the backdrop or curtain.

The supports for the train windows (see bottom photograph on page 126) are painted this way. They could barely be detected against the red curtain.

Another handy scenery item is a mini-flat, approximately 2 feet high and 6 feet long, which can be used as a fence, stone wall, hedge or even a small flower garden. It can help to change the look of a backdrop as shown in the photographs on pages 118–119. Simply cut a piece of cardboard from a refrigerator or other appliance box and nail a 2 × 2 inch board along one side of the bottom edge. Attach 2 × 6 inch feet similar to those used in the flat to the board for balance as shown in the illustration. Make the mini-flat reversible by painting the board to match the design on the cardboard.

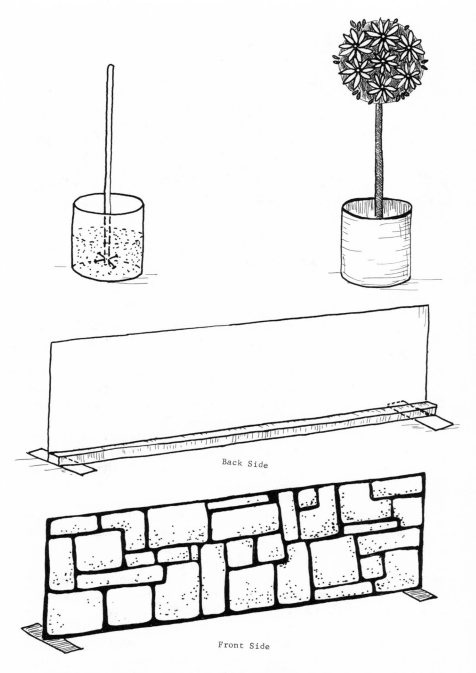

Back Side

Front Side

Top: Canned concrete support and topiary tree. Bottom: Fence, wall or hedge, front and back.

Trains

Train scenes are perfect for performing in front of the curtain. By using a side view, cardboard seats can be attached to kid-sized chairs to create a convincing train. The seats can be arranged either one behind the other or facing each other in pairs, depending upon the type of action the scene requires. For example, if a great deal of conversation between characters takes place on the train, seats in pairs create a more natural setting than having the young actors all sit facing forward and twist in their seats to speak to each other. Either way, two chairs may be placed behind each cardboard front to make the illusion of a wide train seat.

Step 1 is to decide on the arrangement, type and number of chairs to be used in the scene. Generally, non-folding chairs are best if available. Step 2 is to beg some large cardboard boxes from a local furniture store. Make sure the box pieces are big enough to hide a child-sized chair viewed from the side.

Make a pattern by placing the cardboard against the side of the chair and tracing around the chair. Then design the shape of the seat, making it larger than the chair outline. You can build in fanciful shapes and curlicues to suggest plush cushions if you wish. Just be sure you don't build the arm and back of the chair up so high that when the actors sit normally in the chairs, they are hidden from the audience's view.

Cut out the cardboard seat, using a razor blade cutter. The type used for trimming wallpaper is ideal, and office supply stores stock boxes of utility single edge razor blades which are especially handy for projects around the house. Keep them stored away from little fingers, of course. Be sure to work on top of a piece of scrap cardboard or plywood so that the razor blade does not cut through and damage your working surface.

All of the remaining seats can be drawn and cut by using the original as a pattern. Later painting will be easier if you face the inside of the box, the side with no printed labels, toward the front. Some black printing is difficult to cover with paint. If you have decided to use the pairs-of-seats arrangement, be sure you cut half of the seats facing right and half facing left.

Once that is done, figure out what pattern, if any, you wish to have on the side of the seat. You may involve the children in this artistic brainstorming. The name of the train, a floral or geometric shape are among the thousands of possibilities. If you choose an intricate design, it can be uniformly transferred to each seat by drawing the

Top: Side-view cardboard train seats attached to chairs create a convincing look. Bottom: Face-to-face train seats provide easy conversation areas.

**1. Trace outline of
chair onto cardboard.**

**2. Draw and cut
shape of train seat.**

**3. Trace design onto
seat using carbon paper.**

**4. Tape train seat
back to chair.**

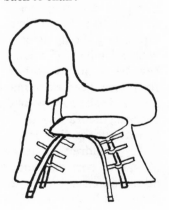

Train seats.

design on a piece of light paper such as typing paper. Position the paper on the cardboard seat in the right area, and slip a piece of ordinary carbon paper between the paper and the cardboard, carbon side down. Then trace over the top design, and it will be transferred to the cardboard. Repeat this for each train seat. With a wide felt-tipped marker, go over the design, and the seats are ready for painting by the children with ordinary tempera paint on Scenery Painting Day.

After painting, during the drying process, you may notice the cardboard has a tendency to curl toward the painted side. Two simple steps should minimize this problem. First, place a heavy object such as a jar of paint in the center of the seat while it dries, lying on a flat surface. Second, paint the back as well as the front, using the same paint, but don't bother with the fancy design on the back. I usually have the back side painted and dry before the children paint the front side.

To attach the seats to the chairs, use your old friend, the masking tape. Use several long strips on each chair leg so that the cardboard front is securely held to the side of the chair. As the actors move into and out of the train seats, they may accidently bump the seat front, and the audience will be treated to the amusing sight of the chair front falling flat on the stage. Make sure you use enough tape so that the seat front can withstand a small amount of bumping without loosening.

If you plan to perform your show at several locations and use chairs available at each, the repeated application and removal of the masking tape may begin to tear away from the top layers of cardboard on the back of the seat. In addition, you may find that your brand of masking tape may begin to tear away the top layers of cardboard solution to both problems is to apply long strips of cloth-backed duct tape along the areas backed by the chair legs where the masking tape will be applied. The masking tape will stick easily to the duct tape and can be removed without tearing the cardboard. During the performance, keep extra masking tape on hand for quick repairs between scenes. Make sure your stage crew has many opportunities to practice carrying the train seats on and off stage so that they can learn how to do so without bending or tearing off the seat fronts.

Children are fiercely proud and protective of three things: their play, their costumes and their scenery. You, the Scenery Designer, have added an entirely new dimension to their play, and they realize how hard you have worked to help them make their play one of the best things that has come into their young lives. They have learned much from you, and knowledge is never wasted in the human existence. You have become their special friend, and a child's friendship is a joyous gift.

XI

Backstage Dynamics

Backstage is the unglamorous but vital side of play production. If the audience is to enjoy a flawless performance on stage, things must run smoothly backstage. It is truly the testing ground for all the planning and rehearsing that has gone on before. While most of the props and scenery are handléd by the stage crew children, there must be adults backstage to maintain order, handle emergencies, control stage and house lights, pull the curtain and other responsibilities beyond the capabilities of young children. They must also give the children important moral support during the performance.

Stage Manager

The Stage Manager is the backstage counterpart to the Director, and she has the ultimate responsibility for everything that goes on backstage. If this job sounds as appealing as playing the underdog in a Christians vs. Lions confrontation, don't be fooled. The job of Stage Manager is exciting and rewarding work. Nothing can match seeing the glow on the children's faces when they hear the applause for the first time and hearing the marvelous things they say about the experience they are having. One boy in total amazement said, "Gee, they *love* us!"

A teacher makes an ideal Stage Manager since she knows how to handle children and the children already accept her as an authority figure. Lacking that, you must find a parent who has an iron hand and a heart of gold. By opening night she must know the play well and be a familiar face to the children, so she must be willing to attend the final month of rehearsals and all performances. Assisting her should be two other adults on each side of the stage, enabling the Stage Manager to "float" if necessary. It is best if her assistants are always the same people but it may be difficult to find cast parents willing to view every performance from the wings.

129

Madame (or Monsieur) Stage Manager, while your responsibilities are basically the same during rehearsal as they are during a performance, your approach to them is different. Our Stage Manager, Anne, has developed this philosophy from her backstage experiences, her common sense and her great human understanding. During rehearsal you must maintain an atmosphere of order, cooperation and hard work. Rehearsals can become tiring and boring, especially to children who must spend endless hours waiting backstage for their cues. Some 10 year olds dream up ingenious ways to occupy themselves at such times. You must convince them that what they do offstage is just as important as what they do onstage. Talking and mischief are unprofessional and can ruin what is happening onstage. For some children a scowl followed by a smile is enough to bring them back into line. Others require more imaginative measures. Let them know that you will be hard on their behavior but not on them.

During the actual performance, the atmosphere is totally different. The children will be nervous and scared so let them know that you understand how they feel, you are going to give them all the support you can, and you are expecting great things of them. Keep everything upbeat. Once the show starts, give a physical sign, such as thumbs-up, to show that everything is going to be OK. When they do something well, react as though you are as proud as they are. If they make a mistake, tell them it is all right. Use plenty of praise and only constructive criticism, such as "smile" or "louder." No negative criticism should be used on this occasion. If you have to make them stop talking, make a funny face so they get the message without feeling stepped on. Be certain that your assistants understand this gentle approach on this special day.

As Stage Manager, you, as well as your assistants, will need a few pieces of basic survival equipment. Your most valuable possession is your specially marked script. During the course of rehearsals, you will note in the margins of your script everything for which the backstage adults and crew are responsible. Using different colored pens for the different jobs, note changes in scenery, costumes, props and who is responsible for them, curtains, house and stage lights, microphone settings, and any of the other 1,001 details that every show has. If a particular job such as curtain closing must be done exactly on cue, underline the last line of the preceding song or dialogue to remind yourself that a change is coming up. Make sure your assistants have the same notations in their scripts.

In our production of *Annie Get Your Gun*, our intrepid Stage Manager, Anne, had these notations in her script for the end of Act I and the beginning of intermission. She had underlined the last three lines of the closing song; then:

(1) Curtain
(2) Darlene—mike—announcement
(3) House lights on
(4) Mikes off
(5) Spots off
(6) Footlights off
(7) Train and Hotel Brevoort scenery on
(8) Indians change costume
(9) 10 minute intermission

In addition to these reminders, work out a signal system with the Director who will be seated in the audience in your line of vision. The two of you will decide whether an extra bow or encore is appropriate. With your script in hand, you will be the backstage nerve center.

You will find it convenient to have a cobbler's or carpenter's apron with lots of pockets. In it you will keep your script and pen plus all of the other repair equipment you might need on a moment's notice to deal with ripped costumes, smudged lipstick, mussed hair and all manner of catastrophes. Include boys' and girls' lipstick, hair brush, masking tape, safety and hair pins, bandaids, small scissors and three sewing needles threaded with white, black and another predominant color thread secured in a piece of cardboard. You may also wish to have on hand a few pieces of 12 × 12 inch cardboard and a felt-tipped marker to make signs to use for signaling the cast, such as "freeze," "encore," and other ad libs as needed.

As Stage Manager you will be responsible for checking costumes before the show. If a child must change costume during the course of the show, it is imperative that his costume be on the side of the stage on which he exits in that scene. Note in your script a complete list of costumes for stage right and another list for stage left. Check and double check them before each performance. Costumes that wrinkle easily will have to be hung on coat hangers. Coat hangers have a nasty habit of turning into a tangled mess when abandoned during a show and making an awful racket when accidently dropped, so try to keep their number to a minimum. Costumes that don't wrinkle can be packed in plastic bags labeled with the owner's name. Other items can be packed in boxes or suitcases. Never use paper or cellophane bags; they are too noisy. During the show as the children stand ready to enter the stage, quickly glance at them to be certain the blouse is tucked in, the fly is zipped and the shoes are tied.

On opening night have a small jug of water and 5 ounce paper cups handy for the soloists to have a sip of water after each number. The rest of the cast may have a sip during the intermission, but only a sip because no one may leave the stage during a performance to go to the bathroom except in dire circumstances and only with the permission of the Stage Manager. Aside from essential costumes, props and scenery, keep backstage paraphernalia and clutter to a bare minimum.

Stage Crew

When you cast your play in December, you will choose a stage crew to be responsible for scenery and props during the show. The number chosen will be determined by the number of your sets and props, but four children have been adequate to handle the requirements of most of our shows. Scene changes should occur smoothly, quickly and quietly. Since a scene can be spoiled by the absence of an important prop, the stage crew should consist of reliable students, ones you can trust never to let you down. Assign two members of the stage crew to each side of the stage. Provide each team with a master list showing scenery and props on their side of the stage for each scene. Print it on a large cardboard sheet in bold letters with a felt-tipped marker so it is easy to read backstage where it's often dark. Props requirements for each scene are printed in green letters to distinguish them from scenery requirements which are printed in black. The master list used by the stage crew for *Annie Get Your Gun* resembled the partial list below.

Act I

Scene 1	*Scene 2*
Wilson House backdrop	Train seats
Mac — gun case	Jake — book
George — suitcase	Mac — newspaper clipping
Frank — gun and holster	*Scene 3*
Annie — gun	Wild West Show flat and fences
Minnie — burlap sack	Ticket booth
Jessie — burlap sack	Charlie — sign

Appoint one member of the crew to act as Stage Crew Chief. Things seem to go better if one person has the final responsibility. It is his job to double check each detail before the scene opens. He must make sure that the right scenery is on stage, that the props are in the right hands and that all costume changes have been completed. He receives a nod from the Stage Manager, his fail-safe system, and then signals with a flashlight to the lights technician who turns on the stage lights for the scene to begin.

When you begin rehearsals in January, emphasis will be on dialogue and staging, and you will use only absolutely necessary props. As rehearsals proceed through February, begin to introduce more props so that the stage crew will gradually become accustomed to handling the pieces. They must learn to lay out each prop, in the order it is to be used, and to put everything safely away after rehearsals and performances. Many of the props may be borrowed items, and their safe-keeping is essential.

By March the uncovered flat frame should be available so that the crew can learn to bring that large, cumbersome piece of equipment on and off stage without a spill. You might even staple a plain sheet of paper on it so that they can learn to handle the complete apparatus without sticking their fingers through the paper. If you used the painted version in rehearsal, it might suffer a fatal case of wear-and-tear before the big performance. Dress rehearsal is the best time to add the painted backdrop and flat sheets.

If your stage has a curtain, it is possible to change sets while a scene takes place in front of the curtain. However, it must be done silently, particularly if the stage has overhead microphones, so that the scene going on out front is not spoiled by noise from behind the curtain. If you have an uncurtained stage, it is especially important that scene changes occur smoothly since it happens right before the eyes of the audience. Since they are visible to the audience, stage crew members who choose not to have acting parts should wear a simple costume appropriate to the show, even if it is only an accessory such as a neckerchief or hat. This may seem a small detail, but it helps to maintain the mood of the show.

Remember that your stage crew members are children, though reliable ones. They need to practice their jobs just as the rest of the cast does. They should develop the habit of using the master list and not rely on memory from the beginning to the end. Once they are accustomed to their jobs, they will perform expertly just as your young actors will. One of our youngsters overcame a fear of heights and learned to install our three overhead microphones while standing on a shaky ladder. After he came down from the ladder, he said, "I was so scared my knees were shaking, but I knew that was my job!" Be certain to stress to the rest of the children how important this job is to the success of the show. The stage crew children must have a feeling of their importance too!

Props

The term "props" is a nickname for "properties" and refers to items used on stage other than scenery, such as suitcases, baskets, musical instruments, books, etc. They add realism to the story, and they can be either borrowed or made. As you work on your script, try to eliminate any props you know will be impossible to find. Then make a complete list of those props you will need.

Present the list at your parents' meeting in October and you will be pleased to find that your parents will already have many of the items at home. From that point, the search will fan out via the parents to friends and relatives who may be able to help. For one of our shows, we needed a light saddle. I knew the weight of a regular saddle was too great for the 10 year old boy who was to carry it on stage. A parent was able to round up a pony saddle for us. Another show called for a World War II Nazi armband, and we actually located an authentic one. We have borrowed rocking chairs, suitcases, a guitar, violin, cornet. Need a bed? Some family is certain to have a roll-away cot. Covered with a bedspread, it is ideal and it can be stored easily backstage when not in use. One of our shows had a western theme. We decided that to give our stage set a "country" touch, we needed a real bale of hay. Luckily, one of our parents intended to reseed his suburban lawn that spring and planned to cover the grass seed with hay, so he bought the bale and loaned it to us before he used it. How's that for cooperation?

What you cannot borrow, you must make. In *Annie Get Your Gun*, Annie is adopted into the Sioux Indian Tribe. During the ceremony Chief Sitting Bull places around Annie's neck a necklace so heavy that Annie staggers under its weight. Our necklace was made from a kit ordered from an Indian supply company and had plastic bear claws and small pieces of rabbit fur attached to a leather thong. Although the necklace looked heavy and our Annie's knees buckled when it was put over her head, it was actually light as a feather. In another play one character was supposed to wear a monocle, a difficult item to find. We purchased a large wooden cafe curtain ring, painted it black and attached a black cord to it. From the audience's view, our monocle was quite realistic, even without glass in it.

The same show called for an oriental gong. We rigged a large brass tray to a stand and the actor hit the tray with the heel of his hand instead of a mallet to avoid denting the tray. It looked as impressive as the sabers in the sword dance which were made from plywood. I drew a pattern on brown wrapping paper of scimitar-type sabers from which a father cut four from scrap plywood which he had on hand. We

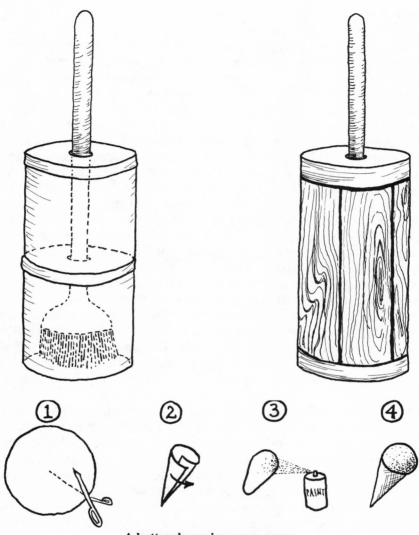

A butter churn; ice cream cones.

painted them gold and the dancers looked dashing wielding such weapons on stage.

The raw materials for most of your props can be found at the dump. Collect throwaways such as pieces of styrofoam, poster board, foam rubber, carpeting, large ice cream containers, scrap lumber. The most versatile material though is good, old, reliable cardboard. It can be cut into any shape, painted with school tempera paint, is self-supporting and available in abundance at no cost to you. The boxes which come on major appliances such as refrigerators are ideal. Cut the cardboard with your wallpapering tool, the razor blade cutter. Handle the cardboard in the same way as that used for the train seats, mentioned in the Scenery chapter. Using cardboard we have made everything from potted ferns to tombstones.

For our western show our Scenery Designer created a butter churn from two 5 gallon ice cream containers donated by a local ice cream store, an old broom and a little ingenuity. She glued the tops on the containers and then glued the two containers together, one on top of the other. The old broom handle was threaded through holes in the containers. What remained of the broom straw at the bottom kept the handle from slipping out. She then covered the sides of the "churn" with poster board and painted on a wood grain pattern using two shades of brown paint and a black felt-tipped marker for accent. It looked so realistic that a nearby high school borrowed it the next year for its production of *Oklahoma!*

A light cardboard, such as poster board, is ideal for props requiring molding or curling. We manufactured permanently frozen ice cream cones from poster board and styrofoam pears. We cut 12 inch circles from poster board, painted them light brown and then cut a single slit from one edge into the center. The circles were then curled and glued into a cone shape and the styrofoam pears, painted pastel ice cream colors, were glued into the paper cones. They looked good enough to eat!

Jean, our Scenery Designer, let her imagination run wild over the finale for our production of *Annie Get Your Gun*. We decided that the finale should resemble a circus parade. Obviously, live horses and elephants were out, but we wanted to give the audience a feeling of the rich pageantry of a parade. The solution seemed to be having the cast members carrying something colorful and festive—but what?

While the Director choreographed a marching finale routine for 16 children, Jean designed something we nicknamed "Flags and Fluffies." Each child would carry a 4 foot stick (1 inch square) cut by a father from old furring strips and painted turquoise. At the top of eight of the sticks would be the Flags. No one ever guessed that the Flags had once been an umbrella covering. A donated umbrella was dismantled and the fabric sections taken apart, resulting in four red and four blue triangular rayon pieces measuring 18 inches in length and 12 inches at the wide end. Jean sewed them into penants, slipping a triangular piece of poster board in for stiffness and tacked them to the 4 foot stick. For interest she added a short thong with four feathers at the top.

The "Fluffies" (top) made a simple but showy accessory for the *Annie Get Your Gun* finale (bottom).

At the top of the other eight sticks were the Fluffies, round card-board discs with fluffy feathers radiating 6 inches out from the edges all the way around. Jean cut two 11 inch discs for each Fluffy and drew a thunderbird design on each with a black felt-tipped marker. The children painted the discs with red and turquoise tempera paint. Jean then glued the turquoise feathers onto the back of one of the discs for each Fluffy. The fuzzy feathers were attached overlapping along the edge with plenty of white glue and allowed to dry overnight. The feathered and unfeathered discs were tacked back-to-back at the top of the stick. The Flags and Fluffies survived countless rehearsals and made a colorful addition to the big finale. The children sang *There's No Business Like Show Business* and marched, carrying these bright props overhead. Their audience responded with wild applause and cheers!

Sound Effects

Fortunately, most Broadway musicals appropriate for children do not require many sound effects. The few that are called for can be handled with ease. A thunderstorm, for example, can be simulated by a stage crew member rattling a piece of sheet aluminum off stage. Church bells can be created by using metal pipe cut in different lengths. String the pipes on a piece of cord, knotting the cord to separate them, and have the stage crew "play" the pipes using a drum stick or mallet.

The stickiest problem we ever dealt with was the gunshot sound effect for *Annie Get Your Gun*. Had it been an adult production, we would have simply used a starter gun with blank cartridges, but the thought of a 10 year old with anything resembling a real gun in her hand sent shivers up our spines, so we looked for a safe and cheap alternative. You will find that many adult theater techniques are not acceptable for use with children.

For the clay pigeon shooting scene, the actors wore toy guns and holsters. Someone off stage would clap two wooden blocks together at the moment the gun was "fired." The actor would yell, "Pull!" for the clay pigeon to be released, and fire his gun toward stage right by simulating a recoil at the same moment the blocks were clapped together. It soon became apparent that the children would not be able to syncronize the clap with the recoil. The children tried using caps in their guns but caps were too unreliable. As mentioned in the Direction chapter, the problem was ultimately solved by changing the audience's view of the actors firing the guns. By firing the gun toward them instead of stage right, the audience could not detect those times when the clap did not exactly match the recoil. The shot was never as loud as we would have liked. Later a professional sound effects man told me that a believable gunshot can be made by using a snare drum. Lay one drumstick from the center of the drumhead to the outer rim. Hold the drumstick tight and strike it sharply with the other drumstick. It is much louder than clapping two blocks of wood together and just as safe.

If you need the sound of a train or something else which is hard to simulate, you may be able to make a tape recording yourself and play it near a microphone backstage at the appropriate moment. Of course, professional sound effects tapes and records are available, and most companies which sell them will send you a free catalog upon request. Keep in mind that tape recorders and record players take up valuable space backstage. We have never had to resort to the use of tapes or records.

Lights

If you have a curtained stage, you will have onstage lights and probably footlights already installed. They will be operated from a control panel backstage by your Stage Manager. Some schools own a large spotlight which must be operated from the audience area by your young lights technician. You are fortunate indeed if you have such facilities, for your lights problems will be non-existent.

The rest of you, who are lacking such wonders, will have to come up with some stage lights, not only to enable your audience to see the show but also to create darkened breaks between acts for scenery changes on your uncurtained stage. To create natural lighting for your actors, the light must come from a source situated as high as possible. Sunlight does, after all, come from above, placing the shadows of the face in the expected places. Stage lights placed at eye level will cause your actors to squint. Lights from below create a ghoulish look and unless you are doing a Halloween play, that is probably not the look for which you are striving. Therefore, if you can find any way to mount lights on or near the ceiling, do it. Your parents may have some good ideas for this.

If that is not possible and if you need portable lights for your "road show," consider our system which has served admirably. For your first no-budget show, try to borrow five spotlights with fixtures from parents and mount them on a heavy 6 × 36 inch board. The middle three spotlights will point straight ahead to light the center of the stage. The two on the outside will angle toward the front corners of the

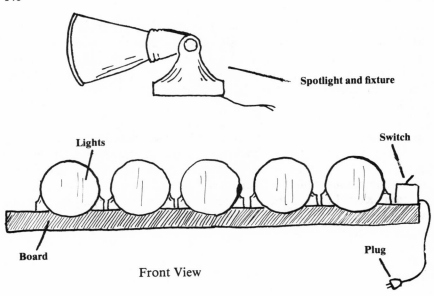

Spotlight and fixture

Lights

Switch

Board

Plug

Front View

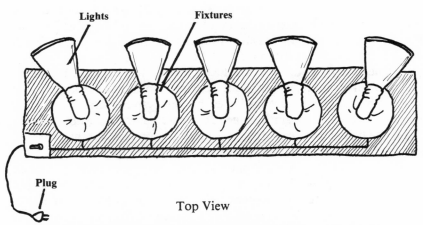

Lights

Fixtures

Plug

Top View

Light board, with five spotlights wired in parallel on a heavy board.

stage. Someone you know may have an old floodlight bar for a movie camera no longer in use and be willing to donate it. Unfortunately, floodlights have a short life span so replace them with longer lasting spotlights as they burn out. Wire the cords to an on-off switch and an electrical plug, both available at hardware stores.

The entire lights assembly board must be placed as high as

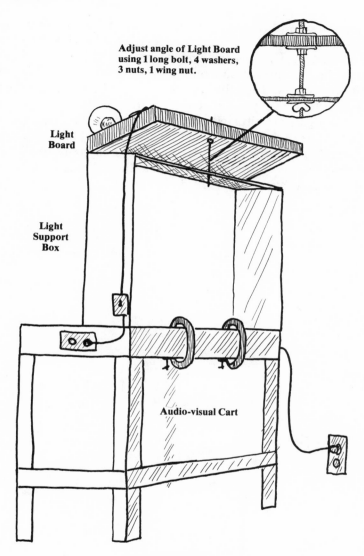

Adjust angle of Light Board using 1 long bolt, 4 washers, 3 nuts, 1 wing nut.

Light Board

Light Support Box

Audio-visual Cart

Full light system.

possible so search your school for a tall audio-visual cart, used for movie projectors, etc., usually 4 feet high, on which to place the board. A better plan is to build an open rectangular box to place on top of the cart which can raise the light board even higher. Ours is 3 feet wide, 4 feet high and 1 foot deep. Borrowed C-clamps secure the box to the cart. As shown in the illustration above, a long bolt with a special arrangement of washers and nuts enables us to adjust the light board to the right angle for whatever stage we are using. The wire to the control switch is elongated so that the lights technician can reach it. The light board is plugged into the plug on the cart and the cart cord is plugged into the wall outlet. Tape the cord to the floor if it is long so that excited youngsters in your audience will not trip over it.

The lights are situated near the center of the first row of the audience. The lights technician sits beside it, the only person authorized to touch the switch. He must keep his script beside him at all times so he turns the lights on and off at the right moments. He may wish to underline his cue lines in red.

XII

Programs and Photographs

It is March, and the show rehearsals on the stage are moving along well. Begin to think of the other things that will go into making your play a success. Every detail must be just right and the children should be involved in those details.

Programs

You must plan your program for the play. Naturally, the body of the program will include a listing of the acts and scenes, the songs to be sung in each and the names of all the children who have worked on the play. It must also include the names of everyone else who made the play possible. Carefully keep a list of every person who has helped in any way over the months. Each one who has contributed effort outside of making his own child's costume must be mentioned in the program. Check and double check that list to make sure no one has been forgotten. List the names according to the kind of help given. If parents have helped in more than one area, list their names under each category. If someone has signed up to assist in a job not yet needed, such as transportation of children or scenery, be sure his name is included. Your play would not be happening without the assistance of those wonderful, busy people, and you want to recognize each one of them. We always add a one-page insert to our program, listing each parent who has helped, and they are always so pleased when they are remembered in this way. I even list the names of non-cast children who loan us costumes or props. Our program insert for *Annie Get Your Gun* is shown on pages 145–146 ("BACKSTAGE ASSISTANCE").

A program design competition among the students resulted in this handsome cover.

Smaller designs can be used throughout the program.

BACKSTAGE ASSISTANCE

We would like to thank all of our fifth grade parents for their help and cooperation in the production of this show. We could not have a successful play without them.

The following people deserve special thanks for all their extra time and effort. Some do not even have a fifth grade child.

Scenery Designer and Artist: Jean Scott
Stage Manager: Anne Ellsworth
Costume Designer: Jo Ann Jefferson
Choreography: Mrs. Ellsworth, Mrs. Dean
Program: Mrs. Jefferson
Backstage: Mrs. Ellsworth, Mrs. Jefferson, Mrs. Scott,
          Mrs. Diamond
Costumes: Mrs. Jefferson, Mrs. Dean, Mrs. Smith, Mrs. Jones,
          Mrs. McDonald, Mrs. Mason, Mrs. Ellsworth,
          Mrs. Rich, Mrs. Neville, Mrs. Daniels, Mrs. Parker,
          Mrs. Miller
Props: Mr. Dall, Mr. Scott
Makeup: Mrs. Jomes, Mrs. Cox, Mrs. Fedel, Mrs. Vance, Mrs. Ferry
Transportation: Mrs. Dean, Mrs. Koan, Mrs. Kubin, Mrs. Toms
Carpentry for Scenery and Lights: Mr. Scott
Diction Coach: Mr. Smith
Photographer: Mr. Scott

Painting Helpers: Mrs. Potter, Mrs. Dean, Mrs. Tesser
Auditions: Mrs. Lynne (our school music teacher)
Financial Support: Cedar Park Elementary School PTA
Special thanks go to our principal, Mrs. Hall, for all her support and
encouragement during the last four months.

What will your program cover look like? It is fun to ask the
children to participate in a program cover design contest. I describe the
contest to the children, explaining what makes a good cover. We want
it to be a simple design in which the name of the play is included. For
printing purposes, the sketch must be done in fine line black felt-tipped
marker, exactly the size of our program. The children may discuss the
contest with their families and get ideas from them, but the actual
artwork must be their own. They may submit more than one entry. I
give them several days to work on their designs at home. Then they are
collected and turned over to our judge, usually our Scenery Designer.
She chooses a winner, and that design becomes our cover. Shown on
page 144 is our *Annie Get Your Gun* cover. Sometimes part of the
runner-up design can be used in other places in the program. We
usually have a drawing on the back of the program to honor another
child.

Since you have the most complete knowledge of the play, the
cast and the parent volunteers, you will type or at least proofread the
program before it is printed. Omitting a name is even worse than mis-
spelling a name. Be sure your final copy is exactly as you want it to appear in the program!

How will you print your program? The least expensive but also
the least satisfactory method is using a mimeograph machine at school.
Drawings do not reproduce well on a mimeograph machine, so your
program cover will not be as striking as it deserves to be. For your first
play, however, you may decide to use this method. Your local high
school may have a print shop, and students there may be willing to
print the programs for the cost of the paper alone. We were able to do
this once. The high school students obtained practice in printing, and
we had a good looking program. A local printer may be willing to do
the printing for you at minimal cost. Be sure to give him credit on the
program. "Programs printed through the courtesy of Vienna Print
Shop."

We have 500 programs printed for each play. We hand these out
to our audience only on the night of the community performance. It is

too expensive to use them at the other school performances. The distribution of the programs is a chance to make four more children with minor parts feel important. These youngsters, costumed and made up, pass out programs on the big night. They are always overjoyed to be chosen for this task!

Photographs of the Show

A cast photographer is an absolute essential when putting on a play with children. So many priceless moments must be caught on film. Find a willing person who has a good 35mm camera to do the job. Since your dress rehearsal includes costumes and makeup, that is the perfect time for your photographer to walk around snapping pictures unencumbered by an audience. He must be sure to include all children in the pictures, no matter how small their parts. He should also snap a couple of the lights technician who is never on stage. If any of the backstage crew does not appear on stage, he must pose them for some snapshots. As expected, he takes more pictures of leading and secondary leading characters. These children participate in more of the action of the story than others do and, therefore, tend to be photographed more often.

Your photographer may choose to take pictures during the evening performance for the community as well. There are ceremonies at that performance that do not occur during any other. Our children always secretly collect money for gifts for the Director, Assistant Director, Musical Director and other adults who have worked so hard to make their show a success. When these gifts are presented, your photographer should have some film left in his camera. Once, our leading man during the curtain calls leaned over and kissed his leading lady on the cheek. There were over 600 people in the audience, many with their own cameras, and not a single one got a picture of that unexpected kiss!

I always pay for the film and developing of all pictures taken by the cast photographer. He is doing all of us a great favor by giving his time and talent to an important job. He should not be required to bear the financial burden of the task too. Since I have paid for the pictures, they are mine to keep when the show is over. I gladly assume this monetary responsibility!

After having all of the film developed, I post the best pictures in my classroom. Meanwhile, I have checked various photo dealers to determine the best price for reprints of our pictures. I then send home a letter, inviting parents to view all of the snapshots and to order those that they would like to have as souvenirs for their children. I have developed an order form for these pictures which I use each year. Our pictures are numerous so I designate each roll with a letter — Roll A, Roll B, and so on. The pictures are numbered A-1, A-2, etc., to correspond to the numbers of the negatives on the rolls. My order form looks like this:

PICTURE ORDER FORM				NAME_____
A-1_____	B-1_____	C-1_____	D-1_____	Column 1_____
A-2_____	B-2_____	C-2_____	D-2_____	Column 2_____
A-3_____	B-3_____	C-3_____	D-3_____	Column 3_____
A-4_____	B-4_____	C-4_____	D-4_____	Column 4_____
A-5_____	B-5_____	C-5_____	D-5_____	Total_____
A-6_____	B-6_____	C-6_____	D-6_____	x . (cost per print)
A-7_____	B-7_____	C-7_____	D-7_____	Total
A-8_____	B-8_____	C-8_____	D-8_____	Cost $_____
A-9_____	B-9_____	C-9_____	D-9_____	
Total_____	Total_____	Total_____	Total_____	

When a child or parent orders pictures, I collect the money at that time. Then the huge bookkeeping job begins. I use a blank order form and tally all the orders, checking and double checking to avoid errors. One year I found that our 34 fifth grade families had ordered a total of 488 prints of our snapshots! This shows how important they consider these pictures of our plays.

Combining individual orders into a master order and submitting it to a local film developing establishment is only half the job. When the order comes back to me, I must distribute them correctly. I use inexpensive white letter envelopes. I write a child's name on the front of each one, and the numbers of every single snapshot ordered by him, copying this information from his original order form. As I take the snapshots out of the developer's envelopes, I write the number on the back of each. I then put them in the appropriate white envelopes, checking off numbers as the pictures are inserted. It is therefore quite easy to see at a glance where any mistakes have occurred, and re-orders can be made if necessary. The envelopes are then handed out to the children in school the next day.

The pictures that I keep of each of our plays are among my most treasured possessions. Every single snapshot has its own story to tell. What precious, wonderful children are pictured there! I will never forget a single one. I will always have my show albums to enjoy and to help me remember!

XIII

The Performance

The excitement is building—in you, in the parents, but most of all, in the children. They have spent at least three months in rehearsal. You and the parents have spent that time on all of the other details to make the show a success. Your first performance will be for the rest of the students in your school. You have cleared the date with the school principal who by this time is almost as enthusiastic as you are.

Have the children bring all of their costumes to school several days before the first show. They will be hanging from the chalkboard, from the window frames, everywhere—unless you are able to borrow a large, portable clothes rack, a handy item. Double check each costume as it is brought to school. If you have a number of identical costumes, such as our Indian costumes, put a large name tag on each of those hangers. All hats, shoes and other accessories should be in plastic shopping bags with handles and the handles looped over the tops of the hangers so that each child's costume is all together. In working with youngsters this age, you will find that many are careless about keeping track of their belongings. Remind them that it is their responsibility to keep their things together. You have enough to do without having to hunt for a stray shoe just before a performance!

Our first performance is usually scheduled for 9:00 a.m. I arrive at school at 7:30 and set up the makeup table in the hall. The girls arrive at 7:45 along with *all* vocal soloists. The boys come in at 8:00. The parent makeup crew is in place and ready to work by 7:55 a.m. We set aside my classroom as a dressing room for girls and a separate classroom for the boys. There is an adult in each, to maintain order among excited children. The girls' costumes always seem to be more complicated than the boys' so I station myself in the girls' dressing room. The Assistant Director is in the boys' room. The boys quickly recover from the modesty that her presence creates. Both of us are armed with safety pins, needle and thread, a hairbrush, and facial tissue. The girls dress and report to the makeup stations. The boys, who have arrived 15 minutes later, do the same. We stagger the arrival times because the makeup crew cannot handle all of the children at once and this helps to cut down on confusion.

As soon as the children who have vocal solos are dressed, they report to makeup and go to the head of the line so that they are made up as soon as possible. Then they report to the Musical Director for a warm-up session. They are due back in my classroom no later than 15 minutes before show time.

Pre-show Jitters

As soon as all the girls are dressed, my classroom is opened so that all made-up children, boys as well as girls, can assemble there. Be prepared for signs of nervousness, especially in your main characters. It is not uncommon for a child to have an attack of diarrhea or nausea during all the preparation excitement. This occurs most often before the first performance and before the evening show for the community. After that, the children are experienced performers and nerves are not a problem. All you can do is make sure they have access to the bathroom and assure them that their feelings are entirely normal. It seems to help them to know that professional actors suffer in the same way.

I remember one shy child who had a dance solo to perform. As the time approached for her to capture the spotlight, she became more and more nervous. Her hands actually shook! With her parents and all those other people from the community watching, she knew that she had to go on—there was simply no way to avoid it. As she started to dance, her nerves lessened somewhat. She did a beautiful job, without a single mistake. After the dance was over and she had exited the stage, her face told her feelings. She knew that she had conquered a huge obstacle—her own fear—and she had done what she was supposed to do. She felt she was ten feet tall! Her pride and her elation were priceless to her. I am sure that child will remember her experience even after she has grown to adulthood.

The most extreme case of nerves that I ever observed was in a youngster who turned out to be one of the most talented children I have ever worked with. His nerves did not occur on the day of our performance for the students in our school. This particular year the news of our unusually fine show spread even before our first performance. We were invited to put on a 20-minute segment for a group of 60 school principals from our county. This show was to be two weeks before our first scheduled performance. We thought we were ready, but we had not had as much time to rehearse as we had planned. The morning arrived and this child's mother called me to say that he had been sick all night long, but was determined to do his part. He arrived at school looking ghost-white! He spent much time in the bathroom, and he was a very sick young man. He kept assuring me that he could perform though. As I led the cast into the cafeteria where the show as to be held, Justin looked at me and said, "Don't worry. I'm all right now." He was! What a sensation he created! Those principals, from high schools, junior highs and elementary schools, sat there openmouthed. They could not believe that elementary school children could put on a production like that and Justin amazed them the most. He put every ounce of energy he had in his 60-pound body into that performance. It was unbelievable! Those principals still talk about it. Justin, who has performed many times in many different shows since then, has conquered his nerves for all time.

This brings up another point. I am frequently asked, "Have you ever had a child too sick to perform?" My answer is NO! I remember the child who was running a 101° temperature the evening of our community performance, yet he did a magnificent job. Then there was a leading lady who went on stage, performed a scene, left the stage, found a bathroom where she vomited, and then went back on stage in time for her next cue. I have had children absent from school because of illness, whose parents brought them for a performance and then took them back home and put them to bed. I even remember a parent who postponed her child's tonsillectomy until after the show was over! Somehow the theater motto "The show must go on" seems to carry over to children and their parents as well as professionals.

The Pep Talk

Getting back to the first performance, have all of the children assemble in your room before going to the stage. You must give them last minute instructions and a pep talk. I always remind my cast members to pause for audience laughter or applause before reciting the next line. I stress superior behavior when not on stage. There is nothing more distracting to an audience than noise backstage. Then I tell them about their audience that day. A student audience of younger children will think these actors extremely good as they try to imagine themselves on a stage, performing for a large group. Sixth graders, in the audience, who did a big show the year before, know the work involved.

They will appreciate the efforts of these children, though they may secretly be hoping that this show is not as good as their show. This is perfectly normal. I urge the children to do their very best, to show the sixth graders that they are capable too.

For the evening performance my pep talk is slightly different. In describing that audience, I tell the children that these people are mostly their parents and friends. If a mistake is made on stage, they will excuse it, understanding that the actors are children. I tell the cast that we want to make that audience amazed at the quality of our show and our actors. I always challenge every cast before every performance — "let's show them we are THE BEST!" And they do!

When the finale ends in that first performance, your children will have a feeling of accomplishment that they never experienced before. This is no exaggeration. No well done school assignment, no winning baseball game, no flawless piano recital can come close to equaling the elation of working so long and hard on a project and then having so many people recognize your efforts with their applause and praise.

Three months before, the idea of singing and acting in front of a room full of people was a scary thing. These children wondered if they would ever be able to do it. Now that first performance is behind them, and they know how good they are! The feeling of self-confidence gained by every child in the cast is something no one can ever take away from them. It lives with them forever, and it influences everything they undertake in later life. You have helped them to achieve it. You know what it is worth to them.

Adjusting to a Larger Stage

The first performance over, the children and adults turn their attention to that biggest of all shows — the evening one for the community. This will be true show-off time! Ours is held on the junior high school stage so we have another job ahead of us — that of learning to use a different stage and its technical facilities. The parents on the scenery and transportation committees must pack up and haul the scenery, props, costumes and other paraphernalia to our new location and set it up for our use.

Our first day of practice on that new stage can be described in one word — chaos! It is easy to become discouraged. The children have so much new information to absorb, and they are so excited that they seem to pay very little attention to anything I say. The thing that is most difficult for them to learn is how to utilize a stage that is more than twice the size of the one on which they have been practicing. Group scenes are especially difficult. The children huddle in small, close groups instead of spreading out to take advantage of the large area. I sometimes put masking tape on the stage floor to help them remember where to stand.

They must also make an adjustment in timing. If a child has been accustomed to entering on a particular cue word in order to reach his designated place before he speaks, he may find that due to the wider stage his cue word must be changed. It is essential that, on this first chaotic day, the entire play is rehearsed from start to finish. You must stand far back in the audience area to be sure that the children can be heard and understood.

You will have to make a major correction in dance numbers because of the larger stage. We have only three days of rehearsal on this stage, and the children have spent months practicing in a much smaller area. The masking tape markings on the stage floor give them something on which to depend and they quickly adapt their spacing to the larger area.

We do not use microphones in our school because the cafeteria is small so the children must learn to stand under the overhead microphones on this stage. A masking tape "X" on the floor under each mike helps and the children are careful to locate themselves at the "X," especially for vocal solos.

Is it worth all the trouble of hauling equipment, a chaotic rehearsal day, and learning to use a larger stage just to accommodate a large audience comfortably? The answer is an unqualified yes! If half the audience had to stand, they would not enjoy our show nearly as much. I would not go to even a professional performance if I knew I would have to stand for the entire show. The other reason we make the effort is to enable the children to use a curtained stage. It is a valuable experience for them. They feel so special on a real stage. The entire environment adds to the festivity of the evening. Even if our cafeteria were large enough to accommodate our audience, I would still choose to have our community performance on that junior high school stage.

Reserved Seats

The parents of our cast members have put so much time and effort into this play that we guarantee them a seat as close to the stage as possible. My seat is on the front row next to the one reserved for the cast photographer. The parents and relatives of our male and female leads are also seated in the front row. For seating of the other children's families, we have worked out a reserved seat system. Prior to show night I take a count from each cast member of how many adults will be attending from his family. I do not include children in the family because they always seem to prefer to sit on the floor in front of the first row of chairs. I then make a large name tag bearing the child's last name for each adult who is expected. One hour before curtain time, the children arrive at the junior high school, dressed in the costumes they will wear first in the play. All other costumes are already hung backstage. Each child picks up his name tags, chooses seats for his family, and places one tag on each chair. He then reports to the makeup room where the parent makeup crew waits to do its job. As the audience arrives, parents and family members look for their name tags and sit in those seats. Other members of the audience must take seats not previously reserved. We charge no admission to our productions, so tickets are unnecessary.

Children who are backstage awaiting their turns to go on should have chairs in which to sit. They are nervous and excited, and chairs help to keep them anchored. You need two volunteer parents on each side backstage to help control the children. If one is busy helping a child change costume, the other is there to supervise the rest of the children. Our Stage Manager, Anne, is always in charge of opening and closing the curtain, a responsibility too great for an excited young child. As an adult, she is better able to judge audience reaction during curtain calls.

Crazy Cue Cards

I am never backstage during any performance. I am always seated in the center front row of the audience where the children can see me and my cue cards easily. During the months of rehearsals when a child made a mistake or needed stage direction from me, I was able to give it verbally. In performances this is impossible. Yet these are children, and they still need my support and encouragement during the play. My cue cards work beautifully and the audience never knows of their existence. In my lap I have a group of white tagboard cards measuring seven by ten inches. I write my messages on these cards with heavy black felt-tipped markers so that the children on stage are able to read them. On each card is printed only one or two words of direction, but the children know what they mean.

My cards read: *Loud, Slow, Face Front, Move Center, Move Front, Sing!, Look Excited!, Smile!* If a child is standing too far back on stage, I hold up the "Move Front" card, right in my lap where my body shields it from others behind me. The child sees the sign and gradually moves toward the front of the stage. Perhaps the stage is full of children and someone enters with exciting news or sings an exciting song. If the children do not react as they should, I hold up my "Look Excited" sign, and they respond accordingly. I insist that my actors and actresses smile at all times on stage, except when something sad happens in the action of the story. After a while, they forget to smile, so out comes the "Smile" card. This card is used more than any other, so pretty soon it produces no results in some children. Then I bring out the drawings of a smile face, and that helps for a while. Then some forget again. So, my next card is a surprise to them — one that they have not seen before. It has a horrible frowning face drawn on it. I try to save this one for the finale, because they not only smile when they see it, but some almost laugh! That certainly adds oomph to the finale! It is always wise to keep a few blank cards and your marker handy for the unexpected situation that develops and needs attention. Once I had to write, "Tell Anne that mikes are not working!" Then there was the time when my sign read, "Brad, zip your fly!"

"Break a Leg!"

Three minutes before curtain time our Musical Director sits at the piano and begins to play the overture. Our audience quiets down in anticipation of the beginning of the show. We, who have worked so hard on so many phases of this play, know that we have done all we can to help the children, and now it is all up to them. The curtain opens, and the first line is spoken by a very nervous youngster. After the first few minutes of the first scene, you can see the children visibly relax. They are having a wonderful time!

A very interesting phenomenon appears at this evening performance each year. Because many of the humorous lines in a Broadway show are not understood by most young children, the laughter at the performance for the school children has been minimal. Adults, however, understand the lines so much better and respond with laughter in the proper places. As the children on stage notice the laughter where it has not been before, they begin to react to it. They come alive more than ever before. They exaggerate gestures or expressions — they become such "hams" that they are priceless! I remember one girl who had a line about a bunion on her foot. She wore a long skirt, and until that evening performance she had simply moved her foot around under her skirt as she said her line. For that adult audience she outdid herself. As she described her bunion she hoisted her skirt halfway to her knee and moved that foot all over the place. It was hilarious and her audience roared! On that evening I always see an entirely different show than ever before, even though I've sat through three months of rehearsals. It happens every year!

As the show progresses, the audience hangs on every word. They laugh in the right places. They applaud every song. They soon forget that the actors are children. They become carried away by the story, and only after the finale is over do they realize where they are and who is performing. That thunderous applause is something those children will never forget. As they go into their encore, their audience continues to clap, finally rising to its feet in a standing ovation to these wonderful children! There are no words to describe the feelings in the hearts of each member of the audience. Can you imagine what those children on stage are feeling? One boy said, "I felt like I was standing on a real Broadway stage." Whenever someone asks me why I put on children's plays, I can only think of that moment when the curtain closes.

After the final curtain, there is pandemonium backstage! Children cry, adults breathe an enormous sigh of relief, and parents begin to come through the curtain with words of congratulations and loving caresses for their children. Belongings are quickly gathered up and loaded into cars. Then all cast members and their families travel back to our elementary school cafeteria for a stupendous cast party with gallons of punch and hundreds of cookies. Children collect each other's autographs on souvenir programs and parents snap dozens of pictures. What an evening!

Cast Party

The cast party is handled exclusively by a parent committee. I am too busy with show details to think about it, and we always have a creative and willing chairman and plenty of volunteers to help her. It's fun to plan a party. About three weeks before the community performance, the party chairman writes a letter to all cast members about the party. She tells them that it will be held in our school cafeteria immediately following the evening performance. All cast members, their families and out-of-town relatives or friends are invited. Each child is asked to contribute $2.00 to cover the cost of punch, napkins, cups and decorations. In addition, each child is asked to bring three dozen homemade party cookies to school on the day of the performance. The committee's job is to decorate our cafeteria for the party, to arrange the punch and cookies on refreshment tables and to clean up after the party ends. Our party decorations are always so festive that the school principal asks that they be left for the enjoyment of all the students.

One year our cast party was made even more authentic by the brainstorm of a few parents who created our own version of a *Variety*-type newspaper. Real Broadway show casts usually retire to the nearest pub to await nervously the arrival of the newspaper reviews of their shows. Of course, our reviews were written and printed far in advance of the party, but the children were thrilled to read seemingly hot-off-the-press accounts of their flawless performance that evening. The review even reported the standing ovation the children had received only an hour before. The author must have had a crystal ball. Our paper included a gossip column with humorous anecdotes that had occurred during the weeks of rehearsal. Each child received a copy as a surprise and a priceless souvenir.

Some Good Things Never End

After the party, the young actors go home and reluctantly climb into bed. They are tired but proud and happy and sleep comes slowly. I have received many notes from parents, telling me of their children's reactions on that evening. One in particular which I will always keep, came from a parent of a very shy boy who played a minor character in our show. It says, in part:

> "I would like to thank you for all that you have done for our children — all the planning, time, energy and work you have put into making our children such a success. I have seen the change in Willie day by day. The confidence, self-assurance and maturing that has come from being a part of (the show). They all have gained so much and you have been the one who has directed our children in achieving this. Friday night after we got home, Willie, tired but experiencing the satisfied feeling of success remarked, 'Boy, Mom, I will remember tonight all my life!' I want to say Thank You so much."

This note always brings tears to my eyes. What greater reward is there in life than to give such happiness to a child?

XIV

On Tour

Your fame is spreading! Your evening performance had a large audience and the community is talking about your wonderful show. Calls begin to come in from other area schools, asking if you could do the show for their students. You have anticipated this in your planning, so you are prepared to accept one or two invitations. To the others, say that you will try to bring next year's show to their school.

Advance Party

If you decide to perform at another school, always send an advance party of adults to the school a few days beforehand. The advance party will check the stage arrangement, piano, microphones, electrical plugs and all technical details. Each school has different facilities, and your team must check out each situation carefully.

Our Scenery Designer is the authority on the "how to" of transporting scenery and setting it up in a new location. The first question is how to hang the backdrop on the new stage. The backdrop gives our show pizzazz so we want to take it with us if possible. If the new stage has a back curtain or bulletinboard type wall, we attach the backdrop with pins or staples. One school had only a cinderblock wall behind their stage so they installed furring strips — just for us! Sadly, once we had to leave our backdrop behind because there was no way to install it in the other school.

The next thing to check on is the placement of the piano. It must be located so that it does not obstruct the view of the audience, but at the same time the cast on stage must be able to make eye contact with the musical accompanist. Check for a nearby electrical plug so that your accompanist can plug in her light. If the piano does not have a light already, she will have to bring her own plus an extension cord.

Your advance party will find places where children can change costumes. Many schools have no dressing room facilities in their stage area. School officials who have portable stages located in the cafeteria usually permit us to create a screen using cafeteria tables, placed folded and upright on either side of the stage. The children change costumes behind those tables. The advance party should also determine where your children will sit while waiting to go on stage. Chairs are essential to protect their costumes as well as to reduce restlessness which could lead to discipline problems. Poor behavior could reflect on your students, your school and your show. I have never had a discipline problem with a cast member when we visited another school. The only discipline problems sometimes come from the audience. Young children, who are not accustomed to having shows or assemblies in their school, have not been taught audience manners. They do not know how to behave courteously. We have seen distracted youngsters talk and laugh among themselves during the show. Once we even witnessed a kicking fight in the front row. Our cast members have learned to ignore such things and to continue their performance no matter what happens. A cast member in last year's show who was performing for such an audience said to one of the backstage adults, "This is a very immature audience." This from a nine year old boy! The adult, while in total agreement with him, could hardly keep from laughing at such wise words from one so young. Our children learn not only how to be good performers—they also learn how to be a good audience. I am happy to say that at most schools where we have performed, the audience has been extremely well-behaved.

The advance party will report all the information they have gathered on the facilities to the Director who then explains to the children the stage arrangement and any unusual situation they will encounter. Then the transportation committee goes to work. It is their job to haul all the scenery, props, lights and extra costumes to the new location. Parents with station wagons, vans or trucks should be lined up ahead of time. The adults transport and set up all of our equipment at the school on the afternoon before the children are to perform. Everything is checked and double checked. All props and costumes are placed exactly where the children are accustomed to looking for them.

Kids on the Road

If our performance is scheduled for 9:30 a.m., the children in costume and makeup are transported to the host school in complimentary bus or parent car pools by 9:15 a.m. The children have a few minutes to look over the stage and locate their props and other costumes. Then they sit in their designated chairs and await their audience. The students of the host school file into the auditorium and take their seats. In order to set the proper mood for the play, our cast members sit quietly until the audience is in place. Then our student-announcer rises, goes to center stage and introduces the play. The show goes on.

Any unforeseen problems that occur on stage during the performance will have to be handled by the children in the best way they can. I remember one show that ended with the main characters walking out into the audience as they sang, symbolizing a journey that they were beginning. As the time for this approached, our leading lady realized that the audience was seated on the floor, elbow-to-elbow, and there was no aisle for her to walk down as she led the other cast members on their journey. When the time came, she took a deep breath and waded into that sea of children, wending her way through them as best she could. As the audience saw what she was doing, they began to make a path for her. Our leading lady saw a problem and she solved it without any adult advice at all!

One year we took our show to a school where one of our secondary leads had been a student the year before. He was very nervous about performing for his former classmates. Because of this, he said one of his lines too early in a scene. If the other actors had continued from the line he said, some of the story would have been lost. They realized this immediately and ad libbed until they inserted the correct information into the story. It was truly amazing!

Your cast members really prove their versatility during performances for these other schools. The way they walk into a strange place and perform like professionals, improvising where necessary, proves just how much they have learned during these months of rehearsals and performances.

Community Encores

One year at least a month after the show ended, we received a call from a senior citizens' home asking that we bring the show to them. We decided to accept the invitation. We had to go back into rehearsal because the children had not practiced in a month. The adults were astounded at how quickly the children were able to bring the play to perfection. In just a few rehearsals, they were ready to perform again.

Those senior citizens loved them. It was a heartwarming performance and worth the effort!

Another year a notice appeared in a major Washington, D.C. newspaper announcing May auditions for the International Children's Festival to be held at Wolf Trap Farm Park. The Festival would be a three-day non-stop collection of acts for the education and entertainment of children. Wolf Trap is the only National park for the performing arts and is located near our town. Auditions were scheduled for Memorial Day weekend, and the Festival for Labor Day weekend. The adults having the principle responsibilities for the show discussed the intriguing possibility of auditioning for the Festival. If we decided to audition and were fortunate enough to be accepted, it would mean summer rehearsals. We decided to contact the parents and children to learn who might be interested in participating and which families would be in town over those two holiday weekends. We also decided to expand our group to include not only the current cast but also a group from the previous year's play. The child who played the lead in that show was supremely talented, and we felt he and his classmates deserved a chance to participate too.

We held a joint meeting of the two casts to tell them of our idea and to determine their reaction. As we expected, they were thrilled, but would their parents agree? We sent a letter home asking who would be in town for auditions, late August rehearsals and Labor Day performances. Just think of the excitement in those homes that evening! Our answer came the next day when the children returned to school. Every single child from the current cast would be able to participate and 25 children from the previous year's show also replied in the affirmative — 60 children in all! Some of them had persuaded their parents to revise vacation plans so they would be available when needed. Nothing more clearly demonstrates the dedication of the children — and their parents — to our shows.

Before Audition Day arrived, the director of the Festival said that she would like to see the 15 minute segment we had planned for the previous year's cast and a 30-minute excerpt of the current show. This would enable her to see enough to determine the quality of the children's work. A quick rewrite on both scripts produced 15 minutes of dynamic songs from Show I and 30 minutes of music and dialogue from Show II, highlighting the best parts and including our "smash" finale. We spent two weeks in rehearsals so that the segments we had chosen would flow smoothly. Though the cast of Show I had not rehearsed in 14 months, you would never have known it to watch them. Even the first rehearsal was superb!

Memorial weekend and Audition Day arrived. Because the school was closed for the weekend, we designated two homes as makeup stations for the two casts. Each home had more eager makeup volunteers and car pool drivers than we could possibly use. The children reported in costume and were soon made up and on their way.

We arrived at the audition site 45 minutes before our appointed time, only to find that auditions were running one hour behind schedule. How were we to keep 60 costumed children clean and well-behaved for that length of time? We decided to take them into the auditorium so that they could watch the other groups audition. They filed in and took their seats without so much as a whisper. Some of the fathers in the group, used to seeing their rambunctious offspring bouncing around home, could not believe their eyes!

I reported to the director of the Festival when we arrived. She was in charge of auditions—in fact, she was the sole judge and jury. There were lots of acts—it took four full days for all of them to audition. She told me that since auditions were running behind schedule, we would be allowed only 30 minutes for our two groups instead of the 45 minutes we had rehearsed. I quickly reevaluated our script and decided to eliminate one full scene and the dance number from Show II. I could not talk to the children in the auditorium so I had to wait until they were backstage, ready to perform, before I told them of the necessary "cut." Our young dancers were extremely disappointed.

The cast of Show I went on stage, and our young dynamo sang with every ounce of talent and energy he had. The Festival director looked at me in amazement and asked, "Where did you find *him*?" After Cast I finished, Cast II took its place on stage, hiding disappointment at having its part shortened and prepared to begin. The director said to them, "If you are as good as the last group, I don't need to see much." They began to perform, doing a better job than they had ever done in any performance to date. I was so proud of them! Then right in the middle of the first scene, the director said, "Thank you. Now I'd like to see the finale." The children simply stopped, reassembled in their finale formation, and proceeded as though they did this sort of thing every day of the week. I could not believe it! Ten year old children! Their audition lasted seven minutes instead of the planned 30.

As we left the auditorium, we were stunned at the way our audition time had been cut. The parents felt their children's keen disappointment at not being allowed to show what they could really do, but marvelled at the way each child handled the situation—like a thoroughly professional performer.

Our Annie Oakley sings *There's No Business Like Show Business* **at the International Children's Festival.**

Now the waiting began. The question was asked daily by scores of people—children and adults, "Have you heard from the Festival yet?" My answer seemed to be an eternal "No." Two weeks passed—no word. Nerves frayed and hopes sagged. Finally on the last day of school for the year, I received the long-awaited phone call. Both casts had been accepted into the Festival! When our school principal made the announcement to the entire student body over the public address system, the cheer that arose from the children almost lifted the roof from the building! It was a moment to savor that I will never forget!

So when the final curtain has fallen, do not dispose of your scenery. Roll up the backdrop and store it in someone's basement. You never know when you will need it again. Though you will return all borrowed props, it is easy to keep a list of them and their owners. Who knows when you will need them again for another performance of your show or even a new one another year. Once a parent has had a child in one of your shows, he will be most anxious to loan you things for another show. There is a camaraderie among past and present cast families—we all appreciate each other and the work that goes into a show. We never lose that feeling of closeness that develops. We all feel part of a very special group that has accomplished something out of the ordinary. It's a nice feeling!

XV

Checklist and Reflections

And so you have it—how to put on a Broadway show with children. We have shared with you our ideas and our hard won expertise. Your creativity will do the rest. What follows is a master operating plan so that no detail is forgotten and a list of those intangibles gained by the children and you. Give it a chance. We wish you luck. The benefit to the children is incalculable. You will never regret the undertaking.

Countdown Checklist

Summer

► Choose and revise the script. Apply for the license to perform your play.

September

► Begin costume and scenery designs.
► Make a list of needed props.

October

► Hold a meeting with the parents of your children.
► Discuss all plans for the show. Recruit volunteers for all jobs and committees.
► Tell children that those who do not keep up with their school work will not be considered for a major part.

November

► Pass out scripts to children. Read the play aloud to them.
► Tell the children what sections of the script will be used for the various characters in auditions.
► Notify your boys that they will be required to wear stage makeup in dress rehearsals and in all performances.
► Try to find a local professional group that is performing the show you are doing. Arrange a trip for all interested children and parents.

December

► Send a letter home, telling parents about auditions, and about costume requirements for the different parts in the play.
► Discuss and distribute to the children the Audition Form, asking which parts interest them, etc.
► Tell girls to consider trying out for boys' parts.
► Find out which children are interested in the jobs of stage crew, lights technician, and prompter.
► Make a master sheet for the adults participating in auditions, summarizing the information you received from the children's Audition Forms.
► Send home for parent signature: permission slips for auditions and for rehearsals.
► Auditions.
► Casting, and announcing the cast.
► Visit the homes of the major characters, to go over their lines with them and parents. This is an optional activity, but I have found it helpful.
► Divide the script into sections for rehearsal purposes. Have the children make the same divisions in their scripts.
► Children memorize all lines during the Winter Holiday.

January

► Buy any fabric that must be purchased in bulk. This could be done earlier, if you have time.
► REHEARSALS BEGIN!
    Children should study lines each night for the next day's rehearsal.

Practice one script section per day, blocking out action, entrances and exits. Proceed through the entire play in this manner. It will take about two weeks. Then start over, and go through the play again.

Audio tape all rehearsals; listen for errors, and point these out to students.

Set entrance cues in the middle of lines instead of at the ends.

Stress the following: (1) Speak in a loud voice, (2) Speak slowly; pronounce every syllable, (3) Use the backstage hand for gesturing, (4) Look at the person to whom you are speaking, and at the one speaking to you, (5) Timing: allow for audience laughter and applause, (6) Do not mouth the words someone else is saying.

► Musical Director works on songs before school, sets up her own schedule of lessons, and posts weekly lists in the classroom.

► Begin to choreograph dance routines.

► Scenery Designer begins gridding and drawing the backdrop and other scenery.

► A father builds the scenery flat.

February

► Begin to rehearse two or three script parts per day.

► Add the songs to rehearsals.

► Begin to gather props and use them in rehearsals.

► Invite parents to rehearsals.

► Check with the children to see if anyone is having any costume problems. Call the parents of those having difficulty, to see if you can help.

► Paint scenery. This will take approximately two hours.

► Around the middle of the month begin separate dance rehearsals.

► Toward the end of the month begin rehearsals on the finale routine. Use regular rehearsal time, since the entire cast will be involved.

► Hold a contest for the design of your program cover.

► Keep a running list of all adults who help with any phase of of play production. You must recognize them by publishing their names in the program.

March

► Move rehearsals to the stage.

► Begin rehearsals at 2:00 p.m. and continue until 4:00 p.m. if necessary.

► Rehearse one entire act each day during the first half of the month, including all songs and dances.

► Schedule a time when your dancers can practice on the stage (we use evenings).

► Add the encore to your finale routine.

► Type the program and send it off to the printer.

► Check with the children to see that all costumes are finished.

► Contact the chairman of your makeup committee, and suggest that she notify her helpers of the dates and times they will be needed.

► Send home a schedule of all dress rehearsals and performances, dates, and times children are required to arrive for costuming and makeup.

► The Cast Party Committee should meet and develop plans.

► Toward the end of the month rehearse the entire play daily.

► During the last week of the month have the student stage crew work with the backdrop, flat, and other necessary items.

April — First Week

► Double check the makeup, to make sure you have everything you need.

► Send home a letter, inviting all cast families to the Cast Party, listing your needs for refreshments. (Our children bring in $2.00 for punch, napkins, etc., and they also contribute three dozen cookies.)

► Find out from cast members how many reserved seats each will need for family members at the community performance. Make up seat reservation signs.

► Dress rehearsals; have cast photographer take pictures.

► Give your first performance for the students in your school.

Second Week

► Rehearse on junior high school stage. Remember that the first day will probably be chaotic!

▶ Do not hold a rehearsal the day before the community performance unless it is absolutely necessary.

▶ COMMUNITY PERFORMANCE:

6:30 p.m.   Cast members arrive in costume they will wear first in the play.

Cast members choose seats for their families, and place seat reservation signs.

Makeup crew arrives, and begins work.

7:30 p.m.   PERFORMANCE!

9:00 p.m.   Cast Party.

10:30 p.m. Director gives a party at her home for those adults who helped her most on the play. This is an optional activity, but we really enjoy reliving a glorious night!

Third or Fourth Week

▶ Take your show to other schools. Send out an advance party of adults to the host school. Have them check the following: (1) Is there any way to install the backdrop? (2) Where will the children change costumes? (3) Where will cast members sit when not on stage? (4) Where will the piano be placed, so that the children can see the accompanist, yet the piano will not block the view of the audience?

Arrive at the host school fifteen minutes before the performance, so cast members can look over the facilities.

What Have the Children Gained?

The play is now over. It is time to sit back and think about your activities of the last few months. What are the benefits that the children have gained from this experience?

(1) They have developed a great deal of self-confidence. Even the shyest child feels that he has accomplished something he never thought possible.

(2) They have learned to work in a group. Each child must do his very best in order for the whole to be successful.

(3) The children and their parents have worked jointly on a project, and have come closer together in the process.

(4) The children have learned to organize their time, so that they are able to handle homework, play rehearsals, plus all the other activities in which they choose to participate.

(5) They have had an opportunity to take part in an activity which they will remember for the rest of their lives.

(6) They will become drama critics with no small skill. They know what goes into making a good play, and they are able to better judge the quality of any performance they may attend in the future.

What Have You Gained?

You have given much; what have you gained?

(1) You have learned to budget your time to a greater degree than before. You are able to balance grading papers with rehearsals, many other tasks connected with the play, and still have time for a home life.

(2) You have given these children an opportunity to participate in a single activity that will influence their future lives in many aspects.

(3) Your ability to assess children, their strengths and weaknesses, has been remarkably sharpened, making you a better teacher.

(4) You have been given a most valuable gift—that of friendship. Those parents who have worked so long and hard with you over so many months have become much more than just parents of your students. They have become very good friends. Some of them will be back to work with you next year.

(5) You have learned many skills that make a good director. You have gained experience and ideas for use with future shows.

(6) You have watched your students grow and mature in a way not often experienced by adults outside the family, even teachers.

(7) You have added a new interest—one that will reach into many corners of your life. From now on you will always be hunting new scripts, new ways of doing things. You have found a new hobby, as it begins to occupy your less busy moments.

(8) You have experienced true joy at something that you have done well. What a gratifying feeling that is!

(9) For what it's worth, you will be remembered by these children as the teacher who "made it all possible."

Index

academics 18, 29, 166
accompanist *see* musical accompanist/
director
actors (*see also* discipline): age 1-2, 6;
reaction to performance 129, 151, 153,
157, 158
ad-libbing 161
admission fee 16, 155
adult help: 17-22, 166-170; accompanist, musical 20, 56-57, 78; appeal for
18-19; author's experience 6-9; backstage manager 20, 129-133; carpenter
19, 21, 105, 120-122, 168; cast party
committee 21, 157-158, 169-170; choreographer 21, 68-69, 168; costume
committee/coordinator 20-21, 84,
92-94, 166; diction coach 21-22;
makeup committee 20, 96-98, 169;
meeting of 17-20; photographer 21,
147, 169; program chairman 143-149,
169; scenery committee/designer 20,
103-104, 116, 166, 168; transportation
18, 103, 104, 117, 153, 159-160; voice
coach 20, 57-58, 64, 168; volunteer
form 19
advance party, tour 159-160, 170
America 31
anatomy lesson 58-60
Annie Get Your Gun: bird-on-a hat 94-
95; Chief Sitting Bull 17, 98-99; costumes 25-27, 84-97, 134; finale 70;
"flags and fluffies" 136-138; program
144-146; scenery 118-120; shooting
scene 54-55, 138-139; train seats 126
apron, equipment 130-132
assembly line, costumes 20-21, 93
assistant director 5-6, 8, 9, 20, 150
audience: children in 155, 160; reaction,

pause for 49, 76, 152, 156; at rehearsal
42, 168; seating 104-105, 154-155, 169-
170
audition evaluation sheet 30
auditions (*see also* casting): 28-32; accompanist for 29; announcement to
parents 23-27, 167; audition form 29,
167; audition master sheet 30, 167;
conflict of interest 30; fairness in 31;
girls for boys' parts 33; judges 29-30;
location 31; participation guarantee
18; rating system 30; requirements 28-
32; scheduling 18, 28, 167
auditorium, small 5-6, 18

backdrop: 15, 103-119; color number-
ing 112-113; defined 103; drawing 105-
110; drawing tools 110; with flat 118-
120; gridding 105-109; hanging 104-
105, 116-119, 159; painting 113-116, 168;
paper 15, 108; perspective 105-108; re-
inforcing 108; repairing 104; shading
116; size 104; storage 117, 165; tabs 116-
117; transporting 18, 153, 159-160
backstage (*see also* stage manager; stage
crew): 129-142; adult help 129; after
performance 157; chairs for actors
106, 155, 170; clutter, avoiding 88, 131-
132; costume storage 45, 131, 150;
counsellor 7; drinking water 131-132
backstage hand 50, 168
barns 104
bed 134
behavior *see* discipline
benefits to adults 2-3, 171
benefits to child 2-3, 151, 153, 157, 158,
170-171